FUNDRAISING
'WE DID IT OUR WAY!'

BY

PETER BEWELL

The story of how a Community raised £150,000
to help refurbish and extend their
Victorian Village School

A BEWCRAFT PRODUCTION

FUNDRAISING 'WE DID IT OUR WAY!'

The story of how a community raised £150,000
to help refurbish and extend their
Victorian Village School.

First published 1996

by

BEWCRAFT

95, Green Road,
Meanwood, Leeds
LS6 4LE

COPYRIGHT Peter Bewell 1996.

All rights reserved.

ISBN   0 9528143 0 7

A donation of 50p will be made to the School for every copy sold.

Printed and bound by University Print Services, Leeds.

This book is dedicated to

THE CHILDREN OF MEANWOOD

My grateful thanks to all those who helped in any way in the production of this book. In particular to my wife Christine for her advice, hours of reading drafts and supplying countless cups of coffee!

To Cathy Stevens for her advice and editing, Clare and Bob Illing, Margaret Leiper and Jacqueline Pallas for assistance in editing.

To Barbara Blakeney, Jackie Brewer, Geoff Holland, Arthur Hopwood, Ian Jackson, Glynis Shaw, Cathy Stevens, and Doreen Wood for submitting anecdotes and the like.

Last, but not least, to all those M.S.B.A. Committee Members who worked so hard during the Appeal and the members of the Community for their generosity and support.

CONTENTS

	FOREWORD	vii
1	INTRODUCTION	1
2	THE EARLY DAYS	5
3	COMMITTEES	9
4	COMMUNICATIONS	12
5	ADMINISTRATION	21
6	COLLECTING	25
7	DONATIONS	31
8	SPONSORSHIP	42
9	RAFFLES	49
10	SALES	52
11	EVENTS IN GENERAL	57
12	SPECIAL EVENTS	
	The Launch	62
	150th. Anniversary	62
	Henry Shaw's 100th. Birthday	68
	Nostalgia Weekend	69
	Foundation Stone Ceremony	70
	Open Days	70
	The Celebration	71
13	AN 'A-Z' OF EVENTS	74
14	FURTHER IDEAS TO CONSIDER	104
15	MISCELLANY	106
16	CONCLUSION	111
17	APPENDICES	
	A History of the School	116
	M.S.B.A. Patrons and Committee	121
	The Professionals	122
	Analysis of the fundraising	123
	Useful names and addresses	124
	Architect's drawing and description	126
	Notes of new ideas	127

FOREWORD

by

THE BISHOP OF RIPON

THE RIGHT REVEREND DAVID N. de L YOUNG
BISHOP MOUNT, RIPON. N. YORKS. HG4 5DP
TEL. (0765) 602045   FAX. (0765) 600758

The rebuilding of Meanwood Church of England Aided School was more than a construction project. It was a great event in the life of the parish and the community. It drew together a great number of people to share in a worth-while and exciting endeavour.

The finished building stands not only as a good centre for education, not only as an enrichment to the buildings of the area, not only as a reminder of the history of the neighbourhood, but also as a fitting tribute to a fine piece of community work.

This history of the project tells the story.

+ DAVID RIPON

1

INTRODUCTION

The 4th. of March 1989 is a date forever implanted in my mind. That is the day that the then Vicar of Meanwood the Rev. Stanley Dodd paid me a visit. Now that in itself was a surprise, since I am a Methodist, and I only knew him to pass the time of day.

After the usual pleasantries, he finally came round to telling me that the Governors of the Meanwood C. of E. (Aided) Primary School were, after many years of petitioning, now able to go ahead with a modernisation and extension programme. Permission had been obtained from the Dept. of Education, and the L.E.A., and it had been estimated that the total cost would be in the region of £1,000,000. Now for a relatively small, and middle-class community, that was a monster sum and seeing the surprise on my face he quickly added that in accordance with current regulations the Governors ONLY had to raise 15% of that figure, i.e. £150,000. By coincidence this was £1,000 for every year of the School's existence. The remaining 85% was to be funded from Government sources.

So far so good. I was certain that the next step was for him to ask me to make a donation. Oh! if it had only been so simple. He continued to beat around the bush before eventually coming to the point. He said the Governors were forming a Committee to co-ordinate the fundraising activities, and it had been suggested that as I had recently taken early retirement, and had business experience, I would make a suitable Chairman. Would I please take on the task? It would, he assured me, only mean chairing a few meetings each year until the money had been raised.

My first reaction was one of complete surprise. Why should a Methodist chair a Church of England Committee? That was my first line of defence, but he soon demolished that argument, saying that it was going to be a Community effort. He also reminded me that there were a number of children in the school from Methodist families, and indeed that my own three sons had all been pupils there!

I then pleaded my second defence, saying that I had no fundraising experience whatsoever, and that running a business was a far cry from co-ordinating a bunch of volunteers. I still couldn't get off the hook, as he said that neither had anyone else on the proposed Committee, and we would all be in the same boat.

Third defence. I said that although I was a Meanwood lad, I had attended 'The other lot' i.e. Bentley Lane, and surely it would be better to find an old boy of 'Green Road' as it used to be known. No chance, I was in post!

So began a three and a half year period of intense activity, which at various times proved to be frustrating, exciting, and stimulating, but above all great fun, and most rewarding. A period when many lifelong friendships were formed, and the whole Community was drawn closer together in a common cause.

By way of a little background, Meanwood is a leafy suburb of the great City of Leeds in West Yorkshire, but was originally a village populated by quarrymen, tanners, papermakers and their families. Despite now being part of a large city it has still retained a village atmosphere, and this proved to be a very important factor in the fundraising campaign. Many of the present inhabitants still bear the names of families recorded in the village at the beginning of the last century. Those who have moved away during the years still regard Meanwood with great affection, and during the campaign we received letters and donations from as far afield as Canada, Tasmania, U.S.A., Germany, and Australia, as well as from all over the U.K.

A phrase often heard at the events was 'My Grandad (or Grandma) came to this school.' We managed to trace many of the old pupils, including one sprightly gentleman who came along to school on his one hundredth birthday! More about him later. The 'Old Boy' factor figured prominently in many events, particularly where there was a nostalgic element, and the Village spirit, as we came to call it, was very evident.

The School is situated in delightful surroundings on the edge of Meanwood Park, with the 'Meanwood Valley Trail' passing close by. It was founded in 1840 by Christopher Beckett, and we were delighted when one of his descendants, also called Christopher Beckett and having the title of Lord Grimthorpe, not only agreed to be a Patron of the Appeal, but took a great interest in all the events, and was a frequent visitor and worker for the cause. His many contacts were invaluable.

Over the years the original buildings had been added to, and altered, in various ways, but in recent times the facilities fell far short of the modern standards required. It was not too long ago that there were still open fires in the classrooms, and outside toilets, so the long awaited permission to proceed with the new scheme was most welcome.

There were many problems encountered on the way however, particularly on the planning side, but that could fill another book! The outcome was that we finished up with a marvellous new school, being a clever blend of the old Victorian buildings with sympathetic extensions, and all the modern internal facilities required by today's education system. A great transformation in a few years from open fires, gas lights, and writing slates, to concealed lighting, central heating, and computers. What is more important, however, is the fact that the School has retained its character, being that of a village School, with a blend of 'old fashioned' discipline, and a religious background. This makes for an atmosphere envied by many, and you have only to look at the waiting lists for admission to see how popular it is.

Well, now that those hectic years are behind us, it has been suggested that all the hard work, heartache, and experience gained should not be lost, but recorded, so that others who may be embarking on a similar task may perhaps gain a few pointers to help them on their way. For other readers it may just be a case of reliving those momentous years, hopefully with a great deal of pleasure.

An important point to remember is that the Meanwood School Building Appeal was very much of a local nature, and was for a specific project. Equally important, it was finite, so there was always a finishing point to look forward to. Other schemes of a more general nature, and maybe on a national scale, have different facets, but many of the fundamentals will, I am sure, be the same, and there will be some little snippets of use for all readers.

When the Appeal was first proposed there were many who expressed the opinion that it would be an impossible task in such a locality, others said it would take 'donkey's years', others said it should not be necessary and that the government should fund it all. Some stated that the Church was so wealthy it should pay, and one was even heard to say that the Queen is head of the Church of England, so why don't we ask her! Personally, though, I never doubted for one moment the ability to bring it off, otherwise I would never have agreed to take on the task, and lead the team.

I thought in my own mind at the outset, that as things in the country were still in the 'Booming eighties' it could be done in five years, with money coming in from donations, charities, and industry in about equal proportions. I turned out to be way off the mark!

No sooner had we embarked upon the task than the economy started to nosedive. Unemployment, or the threat of it, reared its ugly head affecting individuals and companies alike. Things were undoubtedly tight.

On the other side of the coin however, interest rates started to rocket, so that once we had some money in the bank, we were able to take advantage of the situation. I also underestimated the terrific response in all sorts of ways from the community.

The outcome of all this was that we achieved our target of £150,000 in three and a half years. To be exact it was 1,273 days from the official launch on the 23rd. June 1989 to that magical day when we reached our goal, the 18th. December 1992. This worked out at £118 for every day of the campaign, or almost £5 per hour, or 1p every 7 seconds!

I hope that as you read the following pages you will pick up bits and pieces that will enable you, and your organisation, to reach your goal, and that you get out of it as much fun and satisfaction as we all did in Meanwood.

GOOD LUCK!

2
THE EARLY DAYS

For some three months or so before my involvement, the Vicar had been slowly assembling the Committee, and I met some of them for the first time at an informal meeting on March 7th. 1989. This was followed on March 14th. by the first full meeting of the Committee, and what a memorable evening that turned out to be!

There were 13 of us squeezed into a woefully inadequate room. Nominally it was the Headteacher's office, but in reality it also served as the stock room, staff room, secretary's office, sick room, canteen, and general repository for everything you could think of. One thing it did do, and that was to emphasize what a great need there was for us to proceed with alacrity, and have the new school built as soon as possible.

What a start! There we were, in a haphazard room, no table to sit around, most of us not knowing the others, no plan of action, no experience of the daunting task we were embarking upon, and no money. I suppose if you are going to start from scratch you might as well do it properly!

Little did we realise that first night what we had let ourselves in for. Looking back, it is a wonder that we didn't all walk out there and then.

In the event one or two did drop out in the first period, but others quickly filled their places, and we settled down into a hardworking team of about twenty four. As you can imagine, we didn't always see eye to eye, but at the end of the day we were, and indeed still are, the best of friends.

The Committee was made up of Governors, members of the Parochial Church Council, parents, and others like myself with no direct connection with the School. A motley bunch indeed.

One of the first things that became apparent was that the Vicar's idea of 'just chairing a few meetings a year' was way off the mark. In the early days we met as a Committee fortnightly, plus no end of informal meetings in the School, in the supermarket, and the highways and byways of Meanwood. In fact, anywhere, anytime.

The Headteacher, Bryn Evans, and his deputy, Anne Burgess were on the Committee throughout the campaign, and they had a most unenviable task. As well as coping with the everyday running of the School, they had to deal with architects and planners, builders, and the million and one items that kept cropping up. At one stage they had to move the School lock, stock and barrel to share accomodation with Bentley Lane County Primary School which was about a mile away, and later move everything back again. Despite all this they worked incessantly for the Appeal, and rarely missed an event.

The Rev. Stanley Dodd reached retirement age fairly early on in the campaign, and that left us without a Vicar for about a year. He had also been Chairman of Governors, and this post was held by Frank Dunderdale during the interregnum. Frank made such a good job of it we co-opted him on to the Committee when the new Vicar, the Rev. Richard Wiggen arrived. Richard was very keen on education in general, and our Appeal in particular, and said that the fact that the Appeal was in progress was one of the factors that attracted him to the post. He proved to be a tower of strength in all that we did, and a very astute negotiator with various authorities.

To start with we had the benefit of a number of advisory visits from an experienced Diocesan fund raiser, Peter Davies, which were funded by the Diocese, but when these were finished we decided to go it alone. We had a meeting with a firm of professional fund raisers to see if there was any merit in employing them, but after carefully weighing it all up we thought it better to proceed independently. A decision I have never regretted.

One of the first decisions we had to make was what to call the Appeal. This was debated at some length before agreeing on 'THE MEANWOOD SCHOOL BUILDING APPEAL'. A bit of a long winded title, but it told people exactly what it was all about. It very soon became known as M.S.B.A. and pronounced 'Muzzba.'

The appointment of the Officers had also to be dealt with at the first meeting.

CHAIRMAN. As the Vicar had already agreed with me about this post, it was somewhat of a foregone conclusion on the night, but I couldn't help feeling sorry for the rest of the Committee, as most of them didn't know me from Adam!

TREASURER. A vital position to fill. The Vicar had already had discussions with the Manager of the local branch of the Yorkshire Bank, Brian Coulthard, and he readily agreed to fill the post. He and the Bank proved invaluable to us, as they were in the centre of the community, and surrounded by the shops, so that it was very convenient for banking cash from events, etc. It was also very handy for anyone to make a donation, either formally through the Manager, or anonymously in one of the collection jars prominently displayed. Unfortunately Brian had to take early retirement on health grounds, but his assistant Geoff Holland immediately stepped into the breach and served as Treasurer for the rest of the time.

SECRETARY. Another important post to fill. It was recognised that this job would entail an enormous amount of work, and no one was confident enough, or prepared to volunteer for it initially, so rather than asking any one person to take on the task, it was mooted that a pool, or Secretariat be formed. This never really took off though, and we finished up with Cathy Stevens shouldering the burden. She was the Chairman of the Parent's Association, and her husband had word processing and data base facilities at home, to which she had unlimited access. She worked hard and long throughout the whole Appeal period, and was one of the main driving forces behind it all.

The only concession made, was that the meeting minutes were taken, and processed, by Cathy's mother, Margaret Leiper, who was co-opted onto the Committee for that purpose. How she made sense of all the discussions and chattering which went on, and then transcribed them into meaningful minutes will forever remain a mystery! Her mother's presence did, however, cause Cathy severe baby sitter problems more than once!

AUDITOR. Not a post we succeeded in filling at the outset, but after a few months the Vicar worked on Alan Menzies, a professional accountant, and a member of the Church, and he joined the merry band.

PATRONS. The Committee felt it very important to have a number of Patrons of the Appeal. Some well known and respected names would give credibility to our organisation, and their presence at events would also help. Approaches were made to five suitable people, and we were delighted when four of them readily agreed. (The fifth one declined due to an understandable possible conflict of interests).

Lord Grimthorpe. As a descendant of the School's founder he was an obvious choice, and his influence proved invaluable.

Dr. Keith Hampson M.P. As our member of Parliament we felt he was a must. A wise choice as it turned out, as he did much important work behind the scenes when we ran into all the planning problems.

With a Member of the Lords, and a Member of the Commons on board we really were getting somewhere!

The Bishop of Ripon. The Rt. Rev.D.N.de L.Young M.A. readily agreed to be a Patron, and he was not just a name on paper; he came along on a number of occasions, and supported us throughout. One time, in the early days before I had met the Bishop, a Diocesan-sponsored run was organised to finish in Meanwood, so we seized the chance to publicise our Appeal by laying on some refreshments in the garden of our house, Ivy Cottage, which is opposite the School. I was standing near the gate when a middle aged man came running along looking very much in need of refreshments, and wearing a teeshirt proclaiming 'I am an Old Peculiar' (a well known local brand of beer). After a few pleasantries I directed him into the garden, and remarked to a colleague standing with me that he seemed a well spoken chap, and I bet he was a clergyman. 'He certainly is' was the reply, 'didn't you know he was the Bishop of Ripon?' OOPS! I didn't miss him next time!

The Lord Mayor of the City of Leeds. Another obvious choice, the problem being that the individual changed each year. We were fortunate that one of our Committee Members, Alan Pedley, was a former Lord Mayor. Each year he approached the Mayor Elect, and without fail they each agreed to become a Patron during their year in office. Councillors Les Carter, Bill Kilgallon, Ronald Feldman, and Denise Atkinson all did us proud, and all visited the School at least once during their year in office.

****

A LOGO. The Committee wanted to have a logo for the Appeal to use on our letterheads, posters, tickets etc., so we had a competition amongst the children and their families. The winner came from one of the Mums, Kathy Bevons, and was immediately adopted. It was based upon the design of the Victorian window in what is now the kitchen, and as this fronted onto Green Road it was easily recognised by many people, and gave a sense of identity with the old School. An important link.

Well, those are some of the early-day matters which we had to address, but there was still a long, long way to go . . .

3
COMMITTEES

'WHERE MINUTES ARE KEPT, AND HOURS LOST!'

Oh! Not another meeting......How often did we hear that cry. Unfortunately they were necessary, but trying to strike the happy medium between too many, with boredom setting in, and too few, and not getting things done, was no easy task.

We decided early on that it would be impossible to deal with everything in one large committee, so we formed a number of Sub-Committees, each with its own Chairman. (I flatly refuse to use the term 'Chair', which as far as I am concerned is a piece of furniture. Ladies can be addressed as Madam Chairman). Terms of reference were drawn up and agreed by the Main Committee, so that each Sub-Committee clearly knew what they were doing. There were four Sub-Committees that operated throughout the Appeal, and others were formed to deal with specific large events such as the 150th. Anniversary, The Auction, Nostalgia Weekend, Foundation Stone Ceremony, and The Opening.

The early Committee meetings were held in the old school, and when building work was underway, at the Parochial Hall. Sub-committee meetings were generally held in the home of one of the members, with the big advantage of a nice 'cuppa,' one of the essentials for a good meeting!

I soon found out that running a meeting of enthusiastic volunteers was a far cry from running a Company Board Meeting. Orders were out, and cajoling was in. After several meetings, though, it all seemed to gel, and with goodwill all round we made it work. Our Secretary still reminds me about one of my opening remarks at a meeting 'If you all agree with me, this meeting should only take about ten minutes' . . . It finished two and a half hours later!

It soon became obvious where members' strengths and weaknesses lay, and the make-up of the Sub-Committees reflected this as far as was practical. Everyone had good points and skills, whether they were in communicating at meetings, selling goods, selling tickets, writing letters, organising events, manning a bar, or just organising the washing up in the kitchen. All the jobs had to be done well, and they were.

It has been said that the ideal committee consists of one person, but my definition is 'A group of people, each with a particular skill, all working towards a common cause with ENTHUSIASM.' Anyway, we were what we were, and 'WE DID IT OUR WAY'

The Sub-Committees were:

SOCIAL. Chaired by the Deputy Headteacher Anne Burgess, this Committee had the enormous task of co-ordinating all events, staging some of them, advising others on all aspects of running events as required and actively helping when needed. In the beginning events came readily to mind, and they tried to have an even spread, with one event every couple of weeks or so. As time wore on, though, new ideas were needed, but they never let us down, and as you will see later on in the book there were an enormous number, and a great variety to suit all tastes.

Some events were more profitable than others, but with a bit of experience we soon identified which provided the best 'Profit to effort ratio' It was also very important to ensure that we always gave the supporters value for money. By doing so they always came back for more, and an oft heard expression at events was 'When is the next one?' (This was *always* the case at the end of a winewalk!)

Each event had to have a lead organiser, who was responsible to the sub-Committee for the whole event, from inception to the final cashing up and reconciling of the accounts.

SALES. Jackie Brewer headed up this one, and was for ever coming up with new items, and she put in a tremendous amount of time and effort at her numerous sales venues. (Including her own house, which had every nook and cranny full of 'MSBA' goods).

CHARITIES. Initially led by Glynis Shaw, but after she left the district Don Prentis and Frank Dunderdale took over. They concentrated on identifying likely charities and wrote numerous letters seeking help. Only moderately successful, but no reflection on the committee who tried very hard.

INDUSTRY AND COMMERCE. Chaired by myself, we approached likely companies. Initially locally, but on a wider basis later. Where personal contacts existed we achieved a good success rate but otherwise not very good at all, with cold letters proving to be a waste of paper.

THE THINK TANK. Not an official Sub-Committee, but a small ad-hoc group led by myself which met from time to time on a very informal basis, and where ideas were tossed around and discussed. Many came to nought, but we did come up with a few useful ones! The best ones seemed to originate when we were sitting drinking tea on warm summer afternoons under the shade of the big tree in my garden!

****

I remember in particular two of the main committee meetings. One was when the Bishop of Knaresborough attended a meeting in September 1992 as part of his 'Doing the rounds of Parish Meetings.' At the time the Appeal stood at £133,628. The other occasion was in January 1993 when we handed over a monster cheque for £125,000 to the Diocesan Treasurer. I think it could be recorded that they were both rather pleased!

****

In May 1993, six months after achieving our goal, and when the excitement of the fund raising events had died down a bit, the Committee held a 'Celebration Dinner' in the new William Lawies Jackson Hall in school. (I hasten to add that we paid for it all ourselves). As well as having an enjoyable meal we watched Martin Cockerill's excellent video of many of the events that had taken place over the previous four years, and 'Do you remember when we ....' was frequently heard. We had a few speeches of course, and I detected quite a sadness in the air in some ways, with the realisation that we had reached the end of an important chapter in the life of the Meanwood community, and our own lives would never be quite the same again.

4
COMMUNICATIONS

A high priority was given to this vital subject right from the start. It was felt essential that somehow we had to get the message across to everyone in the area what the Appeal was all about, and then keep them informed on a regular basis as to how things were progressing.

Not an easy task, but on reflection, one that we got pretty well right. Before long there were few people in Meanwood (and much further afield) that didn't know about 'The Meanwood School Building Appeal.'

Every member of the committee had to be a 'Salesman' at all times. This came easily to some, but others had to work hard at it and overcome natural shyness, but everyone pulled their weight. Enthusiasm was undoubtedly the main factor, and it really is infectious.

Cathy, our secretary, built up a computer database of names and addresses comprising all the people who we considered would (or should!) have an interest in the Appeal. These were the names of all the parents with children currently in the School, or whose children had recently left, and people on the Church Electoral Roll. Additions were made later as people signed the visitors book, and when donations arrived.

We were constantly adding to the 'Master List' as it became known, by people feeding in information, such as 'My cousin Jack went to the school in the nineteen twenties, and then he emigrated to Canada. He now lives in Ontario and here's his address' In the end we had an impressive list of over 1,100 names.

A point to remember here is that if you keep records like this on computer, you have to register under the Data Protection Act. A relatively simple matter, which only requires the submission of an application form and a modest fee to the appropriate office.

We communicated by various means. First and foremost by personal contact, but also by leaflets, newsletters, press releases, posters, notice boards, Church and Chapel announcements, Parish magazines, and the local libraries.

When it came to the distribution of Newsletters, etc. we devised a series of postal rounds throughout Meanwood, whereby each committee member and other helpers delivered to a certain area. This worked very well, and saved considerably on postage. It is surprising how quickly a distribution covering some 3,000 or so homes can be made.

Obviously we needed a considerable amount of printing done during the Appeal, and we were fortunate in that a local family ran a small printing business, and served us very well, and at very economical rates. Being a registered Charity also meant we did not have to pay V.A.T. on a lot of the printing.

A few words now about the different methods of communication that were used.

LEAFLETS. It was essential to produce some literature before the official launch in June 1989. Easy, just sit down for half an hour and knock out a leaflet of some sort. We soon found it was not as easy as that!

We had to discuss quite a number of important points, and reach a consensus. The following items were considered;

Format: It had to be convenient for posting, slipping into pockets and handbags, and of course through letter boxes, and obviously it had to be economical to print. In the end we decided to have it printed on A4 paper, folded vertically into three. Printed on both sides this gave us six 'pages.'

Full colour or black and white: We looked at quite a number of samples from other organisations, varying from large glossy full-colour affairs through to very simple black and white ones. The former were very expensive to produce, and in our opinion they did not put over the message any better than a simple one. In fact, recipients might well feel we had been wasting the fund's money, so we went for a bit of colour on the front, with black and white elsewhere and it looked fine for the purpose.

Contents. The front page was the most important, as it had to tell the potential reader immediately what it was all about, otherwise it would finish up, like most 'junk mail,' in the waste paper basket. We put the name of the school, the new logo, a sketch of the school, and in prominent lettering

'WE NEED TO RAISE £150,000 TO EXTEND AND MODERNISE OUR VILLAGE SCHOOL.' Hopefully we had caught the readers' attention, and they would open it up and read the rest.

On the second page we placed a brief history of the school, the third contained an architect's drawing of the proposals, and the fourth an article describing why it was all necessary. The fifth showed how the £150,000 target had been calculated, and described ways in which people could help. Finally we listed the Patrons and Officers, with names, addresses, and telephone numbers, and, importantly, the official Charity Registration Number. Each leaflet was accompanied by a donation form.

During the lifetime of the Appeal we produced several versions, one of which was printed in green ink on white paper, and the small extra cost was well worth it. The eye catching effect made it stand out from the usual mail.

The time and money spent on these leaflets was important, and soon after each distribution the cheques came rolling in.

NOTICE BOARDS. We were fortunate that one of the Committee, Peter Smithson, was a signwriter by profession, and he made a couple of notice boards for us. One was placed on the wall of the School on the Green Road elevation that could be seen by people going into the Park, and the other was erected at the bottom of Memorial Drive to catch the attention of people going to the shops. Despite some early reservations about possible vandalism and graffiti we didn't have any problems at all, and they did a good job in publicising the numerous events.

'THERMOMETER' This was also made by Peter, and was erected at the side of the notice board at the bottom of the Church Drive. It was regularly updated so that everyone could see at a glance how the Appeal was progressing.

POSTERS. In addition to the two notice boards, we established good relations with a number of people who allowed us to regularly put up events notices. These included the Yorkshire Bank, Post Office, Library, Supermarket, Building Society, various shops, and a few individual houses.

There was no excuse whatever for anyone to say they didn't know what was going on.

As we were having events about once a fortnight it was quite a task drafting, copying, colouring, and putting them all up, and of course removing them after the event. I find it very annoying to see old notices around and always made a point of promptly removing ours.

The basics of good posters seem very obvious, but it is surprising how often you see ones around with some vital bit of information missing.

> *They MUST include the following items, as well as being colourful and eyecatching;*
> *Details of what the event is all about.*
> *The venue.*
> *The day and date.*
> *The starting time.*
> *The price of admission.*
> *Details of concessions (if any).*
> *Where tickets can be obtained.*
> *The name of the organisation (i.e. M.S.B.A. in our case).*
> *The logo, or something that people immediately recognise.*
> *Last, but not least, use **Waterproof** inks, and a good weatherproof adhesive for fixing.*

NEWSLETTERS. We produced and distributed several of these during the campaign. Andrew, Frank Dunderdale's son, and Jon, Cathy's husband, kindly did the typesetting for us, giving a truly professional appearance at no cost. This saved considerably on the printing costs by having everything 'photo ready.' Each edition was printed on a different coloured paper A4 size, and was headed up with the usual logo, date, etc. and gave as much information as we could possibly fit on two sides of A4. With a bit of thought and careful layout that was quite a lot. As well as the latest bank balance, and forthcoming events, we tried to make it interesting and readable, and in general I think we succeeded.

Newsletters and leaflets were always distributed, mostly by hand, to all those on the master list, and also to other households in the area. To save on costs we didn't use envelopes, except for the few we had to post. They were just folded into three, and popped through the letter boxes. Having trudged round the area delivering a few hundred, I now have much more sympathy for the poor old postman. The variety of letter boxes and their attendant springs and dogs has to be experienced to be believed!

Jackie, our 'Saleslady' tells the tale about one evening when she was on her way to one of her sales evenings, and decided to deliver some newsletters on the way. She had a large concrete gnome under one arm, and a concrete fox under the other one. As it was pouring down she was also trying to hold an

Newsletter
Summer 1992

BUILDING HAS STARTED!

The long awaited refurbishment and extension of our 152 year old Village School commenced on Monday 2nd March 1992, with Shepherd construction moving onto site. All being well, the School should re-open during Spring 1993.

How exciting to see work in progress after so many years of hope, frustration and hard work. A new chapter has started in the history of Meanwood.

Fund-raising continues apace, and although the total raised so far is magnificent, we still have a long way to go. Quite a number of people have said previously, that they will contribute when they can see something happening - now's your chance!

Our target date is to complete the £150,000 target by Christmas 1992, a tall order, but quite achievable if everyone in the Community makes one last big effort.

Finally a word of caution. Building Sites are dangerous, please do not let your children go on to the Site in any circumstances.

Thank you all for helping the Appeal - keep it up!

Peter Bewell.
Chairman, Appeal Committee.

THANKS

To everyone who has supported us in any way at our many events, from Organisers to Washers-up, and Car Park Attendants.

GIFT AID SCHEME -FROM JULY 1992-

If you are a Taxpayer, and make a one off donation of £400 or more, did you know that we can claim back the Tax, making it worth a third more to the Appeal? It applies to Companies or individuals. Ask our Secretary for details.

SUPERB GIFT FROM THE ALLERTON FAMILY.

A magnificent **£10,000** gift was received in January from the Executors of the Estate of the 3rd Baron Allerton who died in July 1991 aged 87.

In recognition of this the Governors are Dedicating the new Hall in his family name "William Lawies Jackson". You can read all about his Meanwood connections in the "Meanwood" book on pages 22 and 23 - copies on sale at £2.95!

A REAL DING DONG!

An event with a difference was held one summers evening when we had a demonstration of Bell Ringing in Church and a few intrepid guests climbed up into the Bell Tower.

TOTAL RAISED SO FAR

£121,000
In the bank

£29,000
urgently required to complete appeal

Perfick!

Did you see the latest series of "Darling Buds of May" and their Christmas Show? If so, you should have seen several scenes shot in and around School. The Filming Fees helped the Appeal Fund nicely.

DEDICATED GIVING.

This scheme started in September last year and has got off to a good start, with many people dedicating parts of the Building, either in their own name or in the memory of a loved one. Details are given in our little Leaflet. Please consider if you can help in this way - anything from £5 for a Stone, up to £7,500 for the Library would be most welcome.

HENRY SHAW
Sorry to record that our Centenarian ex-pupil died a few months ago after a short illness.

Example of a Newsletter (front)

FORTHCOMING EVENTS

FOUNDATION BAR-BE-QUE	Vicarage Garden	Fri 26th June
FLOWER FESTIVAL	Church	28th/31st August
LAWNSWOOD SINGERS	Church	Wed 30th September
BRADFORD CHORISTERS	Church	Sat 17th October
CHURCH AUTUMN FAYRE	Parochial Hall	Sat 14th November.

Other events will be organised. Watch the Notice Boards and "Meanwood Link" for details. *Join in the Fun!* Pop the dates in your diary now.

THE HISTORY OF MEANWOOD

This fascinating book has proved so popular since it was first published in 1986 that we have had a reprint made, and copies are now on sale. The Authors, Arthur Hopwood and Fred Casperson, have kindly offered to donate all profits to our Appeal. Thank you Arthur and Fred.

SOUVENIRS FOR SALE

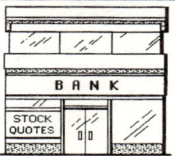

Jackie Brewer continues to do well with the Sales Stall which is at the rear of the Church, and usually around at our various events. Items for sale include:-

THE MEANWOOD BOOK	£2.95
SCHOOL 150th ANNIVERSARY BOOK	£2.00
(OR £4.00 FOR THE PAIR)	
AERIAL PHOTOGRAPHS OF SCHOOL	£4.75
DRAWINGS OF SCHOOL	75p
DRAWINGS OF BELL TOWER	75p
PACK OF 10 CARDS/ENVELOPES	£1.00
MSBA CORK COASTERS 4 for	£3.00
TEATOWELS - MEANWOOD VIEWS	£2.95
TEATOWELS - CHILDREN'S DRAWINGS	£2.50
MSBA BADGES	20p
MSBA PENS	20p

Also various Wooden Souvenirs, Painted Garden Gnomes etc. and other items from time to time.

Telephone Jackie on 741449 or call at "Ivy Cottage".

Despite the Recession, we are planning a programme of approaches to Businesses this year to solicit help for our Appeal.

If you know of any senior personnel in Companies and Organisations who you feel would at least give us a hearing, please let us know *urgently.* A name is much better than a cold approach.

RECYCLING

In the last two and a half years we have raised over £1,600 by collecting and selling non-ferrous scrap metal. Please continue to help in this way.

Leave at "Ivy Cottage", 95 Green Road, or telephone 755415. Items needed are:- aluminium cans and pans, foil trays and caps etc, copper pipes and cable, old taps, stainless sinks, lead and brass - any old gold also welcome!

FOUNDATION DAY

The Bishop of Ripon will lay the Foundation Stone of our New School at a small private ceremony on Friday 26th June.

BUT, even though most of us can't be there, we CAN celebrate this milestone in the history of Meanwood by attending the celebratory Bar-Be-Que that evening! This will take place from 7.30 pm in the Vicarage garden. There will be a Licensed Bar and Disco music to accompany a Cordon Bleu meal provided by Nick Scott at his best. Tickets cost £5 each, and must be bought from Cathy Stevens in advance. There will be a Service of Thanksgiving at 10.30 am in Church on Sunday 28th June, at which everyone is most welcome.

HELP! HELP! HELP! HELP! HELP! HELP!

We have lots of ideas for Fund-raising, but are short of people to organise them. If you can help in this way, or are prepared to help others in running an event, please come forward. You will enjoy it, and be appreciated. New ideas are always welcome.

ARE YOU USING YOUR TALENTS?

Several Friends of the Appeal make and sell various items they have made themselves such as dolls, toys, wood turnings, carvings, marmalade etc.

Can YOU help in this way?

ADVERTISING AND SPONSORSHIP.

Any offers from Individuals or Companies to Sponsor an event, provide prizes, advertise on raffle tickets or similar help would be most

WHERE NEXT?

When the £150,000 target is reached (at the end of 1992 hopefully), what do we do with all the experience and expertise gained over the 3 years? A real Community Spirit has built up, and it would be a shame for it to fade away. Ideas welcomed. Let us know your feelings.

NAMES TO CONTACT WITH OFFERS OF HELP OR TO OBTAIN FURTHER DETAILS, TICKETS ETC.

Revd.. Richard Wiggen, The Vicarage, Tel. 757885
Peter Bewell, Chairman, Tel. 755415
Geoff Holland,Treasurer, Yorkshire Bank,Tel. 741132
Cathy Stevens, Secretary, Tel. 674569
Bryn Evans, Headteacher, Tel. 755883 (school)
 or Tel. 755978 (home)

Example of a Newsletter (back)

17

umbrella and keep the letters dry. Not too bad until she came to a particularly stiff flap when she had to try and push the letter right in. The problem was that the dog on the other side didn't want to receive a letter, but took a fancy to her finger! The outcome was some first aid from the neighbour, followed by a trip to the Health Centre for a nasty jab, and a quick dash to the sale. She arrived late, but sold the gnome and the fox. How is that for dedication? She still proudly displays what she calls 'My M.S.B.A. scar.'

LETTERS TO PARENTS. In addition to the general distribution of leaflets and newsletters, we frequently sent out letters via the School, publicising events, and generally keeping Parents up to date with the Appeal.

CHURCH AND CHAPEL MAGAZINES. Every issue contained all the latest M.S.B.A. news, and details of forthcoming events.

LETTER HEADS. To create a good impression when writing appeal letters, it was essential that we had a supply of printed letter heads. That was another little job that took longer than anticipated. Important to get it right of course, including the correct order for listing the Patrons, putting in the charity number, and the all-important names, addresses, and telephone numbers of the Headteacher, Secretary and Treasurer for enquiry and donation purposes.

LAPEL BADGES and ARMBANDS. It was important for people at certain events to identify the members of the Committee, so we had name badges printed. Where Stewards and Marshals were on duty they wore distinctive armbands.

THE TIME CAPSULE. As well as communicating with today's people we thought why not communicate with the people in the future? The idea of a time capsule is not a new one by any means, but we decided to make one. Now that posed the first question. How do you make a container to withstand corrosion and burial for a hundred years? The second poser was what to put into it.

We solved the first one by talking nicely to one of our local tradesmen who constructed a stout cylinder out of the heavy plastic piping that is used in underground pipes. It was about two feet long, and eight inches in diameter with one end welded on, and the other loose for us to seal when the contents were all inside.

The second brought forth a multitude of suggestions, and we finished up putting in the following;

> A selection of newspapers of the day (The Times, The Financial Times, The Yorkshire Post, The Yorkshire Evening Post, and a special edition 'Leeds, Then, and Now.'
> A School Prospectus for 1992/3.
> The Schools 150th. Anniversary Brochure.
> Various M.S.B.A. leaflets, newsletters, notices, etc.
> The Hopwood/Casperson history book 'Meanwood.'
> A letter specially written by the Lord Mayor.
> A Leeds City Brochure 'Celebration City Leeds 1893-1993.'
> The Citizens' Charter. First Report 1992.
> The combined magazine of the Meanwood Churches 'LINK.'
> An M.S.B.A. Greeting card showing the drawing of the School.
> A Standard M.S.B.A. event ticket.
> Current leaflets from the Yorkshire Bank.
> Scrolls containing the names of all the children in the School.
> Autographs of all the people who paid 50p. for the privilege!
> A Raffle Ticket. (Prize already claimed!)
> A young persons' magazine 'Fast Forward.'
> A Passport, and a Driving Licence.
> Shopping leaflets, and price lists.
> A Teatowel with all the children's drawings on.
> A set of current postage stamps.
> A set of current coins of the Realm.
> A Selection of photographs of the rebuilding work.
> A few acorns collected from local oaks (Will they grow in 100 years?)
> Wooden souvenirs made from old school timbers.
> An M.S.B.A. coaster, and a lapel badge.

It was quite a job fitting them all in the cylinder, but we managed it, enclosing them all in plastic as an extra precaution, and then carefully sealing the end. Written boldly on the outside was 'DO NOT OPEN BEFORE 2093. '

The next question was where to place it? Suffice it to say here that the site foreman, together with Anne Burgess, Cathy Stevens and myself went one evening after school hours to the chosen spot, and saw it well and truly placed and buried. The position is recorded in the School Logbook, with the request that it not be touched for at least a hundred years.

How fascinating it will be for those in the future who uncover it and delve into its contents. I wonder what they will think about our efforts in raising the money and rebuilding the School in 1993, and what will be the state of the School, Country and the World at that time?

I will never find out, but it is just possible that some of today's scholars will still be around then. Medical science is making great strides. Who knows??????

THE MEDIA. We sent quite a number of press releases out to the local newspapers, radio and television. These were quite successful, and we had good coverage, particularly in the papers. It proved again how important it was to have good contacts.

5
ADMINISTRATION

FINANCE. We were dealing with Public Funds and it was essential that strict financial controls were laid down at the start, so in conjunction with the Treasurer and Auditor, a set of 'Rules' was drafted, and agreed by the Committee.

The first task was to open a Bank account at the local branch of the Yorkshire Bank, and this required the passing of a resolution by the Main Committee. A Mandate was drawn up with five authorised signatories, any two of which could sign cheques.

Forms were drafted and printed, so that whoever was in charge of a particular event, or sales function, could record all their income and expenditure. These together with receipts would then be submitted to the Treasurer to reconcile with bankings. To be honest we struggled a bit with this one, not because of any doubts about members' honesty, but because of aversion to paper work!

In accordance with the 1960 Charities Act we had to be registered to achieve what is known as Charitable Status. The Rev. Stanley Dodd on discussing the matter with the Diocesan Treasurer, discovered that we could use the Diocesan registration and use their number for our Appeal. This saved us a lot of formalities and meant we immediately had that very important number to put on all our literature. The main advantage of Charitable Status was that it enabled us to reclaim considerable tax rebates from the Chancellor of the Exchequer, and also gave credibility to the Appeal. It also imposed strict financial controls and annual audited accounts had to be produced.

The Treasurer was obviously in charge of these matters, but with the limited amount of time at his disposal, Cathy our Secretary shouldered a lot of the work, and made sure everything was in apple pie order. She kept meticulous records, and these were particularly important when it came to writing up the

Book of Dedications at the end of the Appeal. She also made sure that every identifiable donor, large and small, received a letter of thanks prepared by her, and signed by the Treasurer, and, in the case of Covenanted Donations, processed the necessary documentation through the Diocesan Office to secure the substantial tax rebates.

As the funds started to build up we had to look very carefully at what interest could be earned, and where. This was reviewed on a frequent basis to keep abreast of the rapidly fluctuating rates. At times the funds were invested in the short term money market through the Bank, but for much of the time the most advantageous place was a special charities' deposit account operated by the Leeds and Holbeck Building Society. We were very fortunate in hitting a period of extremely high interest rates, and at one time, when we had substantial deposits, we were benefiting to the tune of 14.25% p.a. which was a big source of income.

With these excellent interest rates it was essential that as soon as any income was received, either from donations, sales, or events, etc. it was banked immediately. When we had large sums of cash such as at the big events, we had to be very security-conscious. At the end of the auction for example we had over £3,000 in hand late on a Saturday evening. Safe deposit wallets were obtained from the bank and the cash popped in the night safe. The journey from the Hall to the Bank, although only a quarter of a mile or so, always seemed a lot longer at midnight according to Cathy!

One or two people suggested we would do better by playing the Stock Market with the funds. This was considered by the Committee, but firmly rejected. We had been entrusted with public money for a specific purpose, and it was felt that we should not take any risks whatsoever, but ensure that every penny was 100% secure.

Another factor that worked to our advantage in the long run, was the delay in the planning application for the School. This was extremely distressing at the time, but it meant that we were able to keep the fund raising in front of the expenditure all the time. I feel it would have been much more difficult raising money once the building work had been completed.

INSURANCE. An important item that had to be arranged. The policy was dealt with by the Ecclesiastical Insurance Company, and covered Public and Personal Liability. It was never claimed upon, but was reassuring, and essential, had something gone wrong. Although many of the events were outdoors we did not take out a 'Pluvius' cover for inclement weather, but thankfully we never had an event spoiled.... Someone up there loved us!

TRAINING. The Directory of Social Change is an organisation with a bit of a mysterious and perhaps misleading name. It is however an excellent source of all sorts of help for charity fund raisers. Amongst other things they run a variety of training courses, and I attended one for two days in Newcastle called 'Effective Fund Raising.' At the time M.S.B.A. had been up and running just over a year, and it was very gratifying to hear that a lot of what we had done was along the right lines, but there were, of course, quite a lot of other tips which I picked up.

What did come as a bit of a shock to me was that out of the two dozen or so participants only two of us were volunteers, all the others being professional fund raisers (and well paid at that), and I was the only one to pay the fee of £60 out of my own pocket! Never mind, it was all in a good cause. It made me realise how fortunate we were in Meanwood in having a complete team of volunteer workers. We paid nobody!

The organisation also sells quite a number of very useful publications on Company giving, charitable trusts, etc. and several other useful books and leaflets. Their address is in the Appendices.

VISITORS' BOOK. We purchased a good hardback book, and displayed it at all the functions, with the request that all visitors signed. This was one way that we enlarged our data base of supporters' names and addresses. It is also an excellent record of the events, and now resides in the school archives, and will no doubt become more interesting as the years roll on. It continues to be used on important occasions.

It would have been fascinating to find such a book from the last century, but alas we did not.

LICENCES. Applications had to made for a variety of licences. For example, whenever we wanted to sell intoxicating liquor we had to submit an application to the Magistrates several weeks before the event and this involved a small fee.

Details of the venue, date, times, and the name of the person in charge had to be given, and then the police checked to ensure all was in order. Cathy tells the tale about one evening when things had been particularly hectic at home. She was bathing two small children and the phone had never stopped ringing. It rang yet again, and in desperation she answered 'Battersea Dogs' Home'.... 'I hope not' said the caller. 'This is Inspector ***** , and I want to discuss your liquor licence application.' Incidentally, these temporary licences are rationed to four per organisation per year.

A Local Authority licence had also to be obtained to run large raffles and lotteries when tickets were being sold to the public. The fee probably varies depending upon which Authority is dealing. In our case it was £17.50 per year from Leeds. When contemplating a lottery or raffle remember this item. A small raffle where tickets were sold at an event, and the draw took place the same day or evening did not require a licence in Leeds.

A Car Boot Sale or Table Top Sale also required a special one-off licence, and this cost £60, and was limited to one per year of either.

Finally on this subject it is worth noting that although we did not have one, a licence is required to hold any form of street collection or flag day.

6
COLLECTING

It was quite surprising how many different things we collected and turned into cash. Before starting any collection we had to consider a few factors. First and foremost, was there a ready market for the items concerned? Secondly, who would pay the best price? These were checked at the outset, but we had to keep an eye on the markets, as rates fluctuated considerably, particularly on scrap metals.

Where would the items be stored, and who would sort them out and bag them? Was there someone available to transport them to the point of sale? We tried to get one person to be responsible for each type of collection, but more often than not the answer to these questions was Ivy Cottage, and Mr. & Mrs. B!

Here are some of the items we collected;

CASH. The best item of the lot! I started by going to the local sweetshop and obtaining a number of large plastic sweet jars. I removed the labels, cut slots in the lids, placed suitable bold notices on each one, and we were in business!

I approached the local Bank, Building Society, Post Office, Supermarket, and various shops, and they all readily agreed to display them in prominent positions. The Church, Chapel, and School each took one. Beverley Priestley, one of the Mums with pre-school age children, took on the task of emptying them, and banking the proceeds at regular intervals. She also made sure that each holder received an official receipt to display to the public. An important point. She never emptied them completely, though, as it always looked better to have something in each jar. Priming the pumps! This little exercise brought in £375.

We also made a point of always having at least one donation jar prominently displayed at all the events. Never miss a chance.

Another very simple way of collecting cash was the 'Smartie Tube Scheme' that was run from School by Bryn Evans. Very popular with the children as you can well imagine. All Bryn had to do was buy a load of Smartie tubes wholesale, and then give them away to all the children, Committee Members, and anyone else we could persuade to take one. All they had to do was eat the contents, and then fill up the tube with coins and return it to school. They would then be given another tube of Smarties. Repeat indefinitely! Generally they came back full of pennies or twenty pence pieces, but on occasions pound coins were squeezed in, and at least once a rolled up banknote appeared in a tube. This was a real moneyspinner, and lasted for years, bringing in hundreds of pounds.

ACORNS. Yes, Acorns, those little brown things that fall off oak trees! Cathy, our ever watchful Secretary, came to me one day in September and said had I seen the advertisement in the local paper where someone was offering £3 per 2 gallon bucketful of good fresh acorns delivered to a farm near Tadcaster, (which is about 15 miles away). I must admit I had seen it, but dismissed the possibility as I could not see much mileage in scratting round on hands and knees trying to collect goodness knows how many of the things to fill a bucket and then cart them all the way to Tadcaster for £3.

As usual Cathy won the day and persuaded me to at least give it a try. When I announced it at an event shortly afterwards I had great difficulty in stopping the laughter and persuading the audience it was a genuine affair.

Anyway the outcome was that to start with, a few of us went into the woods and made a start. Fortunately for us the woods in Meanwood are nearly all oak trees, so we did not have far to search. We soon found it addictive, a bit like doing a jigsaw when you always want to do a bit more! Martin Cockerill kindly agreed to run them over to the farm in his minibus, and sell them for us. Lo and behold he returned with a fistful of banknotes. To be precise £159! (There is something about getting cash rather than a cheque, it seems much more realistic!) That was it, we were hooked.

It was obviously a short season, as they had to be collected while still fresh, so we had to work quickly and publicise it. I established a number of collection points around the area, and each one had a prominent notice, plastic bags for collectors, and a couple of plastic dustbins to put them all in. I went to a local bakery and they kindly gave me a load of 2 gallon used plastic buckets with lids that were very useful for storage and transportation. The main collection point as usual was at Ivy Cottage, and as this was on the route to the park and woods, we had quite a number of total strangers helping with the collecting, although some of the dog walkers complained that the dogs objected to standing around so much whilst their owners were busy picking up acorns!

The only problem with the storage was keeping the squirrels at bay. They proved troublesome, chewing through plastic with relish, so everything had to be carefully covered each night. We only received one complaint, and that was from a lady who accused us of stealing all the poor squirrels' food supplies, but we politely pointed out that there were still untold millions around, and we did not really think they would notice the absence of the few we had taken. I certainly did not feel guilty.

As usual we kept everyone updated with progress, and so as to give people an idea of how many we had collected, I counted out how many acorns there were in one 2 gallon bucketful (1,829) and then multiplied that by the number of bucketfuls sold. One little old lady heaped great praise on me for 'counting all those millions of acorns' I did not enlighten her as to my simple method!

In the first fifteen days of that first collection in 1990 we collected 328,000 acorns which brought in £525. Manna from heaven. The farm that took them all used them for forestry planting schemes in the Tadcaster area, and we were told that our contribution planted an area of about 10 acres.

The crop from the oaks varied considerably from season to season and despite putting in as much effort the next year we only made £211. The following year they came good again and we benefited to the tune of £511.

Very much a case of opportunism. Keep your eyes open all the time, and even if an idea sounds daft, it may be worth a try.

AUTOGRAPHS. One idea that raised quite a lot of money, and at the same time created a wonderful souvenir was an autographed tablecloth. A plain white cloth was bought from a needlework shop, together with a special black pencil that would wash out afterwards.

The cloth was displayed at many of the functions, and people invited to autograph it for 50p. a time. The Lord Mayor and The Lady Mayoress started it off, followed by the Bishops of Ripon and Knaresborough, and they were followed by about 400 others. All the names, and the school crest were then embroidered in colour by some of the ladies, and the finished result is fascinating. It is now shown on special occasions, and always has a crowd around it eager to find either their own name or one of their family. Another item that will become more and more interesting as time goes by.

'ANTIQUES'. As the interior of the old school was going to be ripped out in the modernisation process I approached the architect, and obtained his

permission to take out any of the fittings and sell them for the Appeal. I identified some old pine Victorian cupboards, some fireguards, and some cast iron fireplaces as likely moneymakers, and asked a couple of respectable dealers to tender. They did so, and we were a few hundred pounds nearer the target.

I also watched carefully the items that came in during the scrap metal collection, jumble sales, and the carboot sale. It was quite surprising some of the items that appeared. I then sold them to a dealer who always gave us a good price in view of where the money was going.

GROCERY COUPONS. These were collected at the school and redeemed at the shops. The cash saved on the shopper's bills being donated to M.S.B.A. Though not a big moneyspinner, it was another case of every little help.

PAPER. We considered this, but in view of the fact that the local Scouts had being doing this for a number of years we did not want to spoil their pitch. It is a market where the price fluctuates enormously, but can be lucrative.

PETROL COUPONS. This proved to be a very good one. We let it be widely known that we were collecting these, and Ian Jackson took on the job of sorting and redeeming them. The gifts were stored by him, and used as raffle prizes and competition prizes. They were quite substantial, ranging from colour televisions downwards. At one period we were allowed to have a coupon collecting box on the counter at a large filling station, and this brought in a considerable amount. Unfortunately the management changed after a few months, and we lost a nice little earner. It was a good example of painless collecting from neighbours and work colleagues, as well as from supporters like Aunt Mary in Aberdeen!

POSTAGE STAMPS. Another painless way of collecting. It is surprising how quickly you can fill a binliner with used stamps if everybody does their bit. Not a big earner, but worth doing. Before selling them in bulk, a local stamp collector would go through the pile and buy any particularly interesting ones.

SCRAP METAL. This was the big one. It took a lot of time and effort, but in the end we were better off to the tune of £1,910.

We only collected non-ferrous metals, as we could not cope with the handling and transportation of big items like Grandma's old cooker.

Aluminium. This was the best one, as there were millions of drinks cans littering the countryside and streets, and also at that time the attendant ring pulls were all over the place. Unfortunately there were also a fair percentage of steel cans around, and they had to be sorted out from the aluminium ones. This was a laborious job, and usually carried out by my long suffering wife with a large magnet. They then had to be squashed, and bagged before being hauled down to the scrapyard.

I do not know how many we finally collected, but it was an enormous amount, and they came from all over the place, including one lot that was brought down from Scotland by friends of the Hopwoods!

The fact that we were also cleaning up the environment encouraged people to collect. Ours were sold to the local scrap man, but there are now special depots run by Alcan that take them in and give a better price.

Another important source of aluminium was old cooking pans, kettles and the like. There was a lot of publicity at the time about poisoning from these utensils, and this worked very much in our favour! All I had to do was knock off the steel or wooden handles, and there was a nice weight of aluminium to cash in.

Brass. The old Yorkshire saying that 'Where there's muck there's brass' was altered slightly to 'Where there's brass there's cash.' The main source of this metal was in pipe fittings and taps. Although taps appear to be chrome, they are in fact solid brass, and well worth saving. Keep your eyes and ears open for people having a new bathroom or kitchen, and speak nicely to them.

Copper. Copper came mainly from old pipes, but some also from the copper wire in old electric motors, albeit rather laborious to extract.

Electric cables. Most came from people having their houses rewired, and from leads cut from old appliances. The best price is obtained if you can take the time to strip off the outer coverings. Note that the old fashioned method of doing this by burning it off is now illegal! Another case of all bits being gratefully received.

Foil. Lots of frozen meals, etc. now come in aluminium foil trays, and they proved to be well worth collecting, together with milk bottle tops. Do persuade people to wash them out first though, otherwise they stink!

Lead. Very heavy metal, and it does not take a lot to produce worthwhile amounts. Sources were mainly from old pipes, and flashings off roofs, (not the Church!) and to a lesser extent from the outer covering of old cables.

Silver. One person brought in a lot of silver shields and plaques from an old defunct organisation, so these were promptly taken and sold to the local jeweller

Stainless steel. The main source here were old sink tops. It was surprising how many turned up. Some cutlery was also brought in. (Keep an eye open for the silver ones).

Scrap is undoubtedly a much sought after commodity as was illustrated to me one day. A Company I knew rang up and said they would let me have a vanload of old electric cable for the Appeal. I thanked them and agreed that they could drop it in the Chapel carpark at a certain time. I duly turned up to deal with it about half an hour later than I had said, only to find two doubtful looking characters loading up the last pieces onto their horse and cart! When challenged, they boldly declared 'A man in Headingley said we could have it'. I quickly enlightened them, and threatened to telephone the police unless they unloaded it in double quick time. Thankfully they did so!

7

DONATIONS

GENERALLY. Without a doubt fund raising is a very competitive business, with many good causes throughout the country, and indeed the world, all competing for a fairly fixed amount of cash available. It was therefore vital that when soliciting donations we had to try and stand out from the crowd.

How to do this was a matter we had to consider carefully. Our Appeal was obviously of a local nature, so it was thought to be a waste of time trying to obtain donations from afar, unless of course there was a Meanwood connection.

Individuals, Charities, and Industry/Commerce each required a different approach, although there were a number of common factors. In all our approaches we stressed that the Appeal was being run entirely by volunteers, and that virtually all the money donated would be directly used for the building work and not swallowed up by heavy administrative costs. In fact our overheads at the end of the day were only about 2%, way below that of the main national and international charities. This was attributable to the volunteer labour, and also the fact that none of them even claimed any expenses. (A fact confirmed by many a telephone bill!)

We clearly stated why the money had to be raised, and always gave the most up-to-date information on the money raised so far, and how the project was progressing. An open invitation was extended to everyone to come and see the work as it progressed, and of course we gave encouragement to join in the many events.

It has been said that the 'Great British Public' are by nature generous, and I would generally agree. We were frequently pleasantly surprised at the responses we received. All donations were welcomed, but it was often the smaller ones that gave the most pleasure. There was the little old lady who came up to my wife in the supermarket, and pressed a five pound note into her hand, saying 'To help the new School luv.' Another nice touch was the little plastic bags that arrived anonymously several times, and were full of coppers. The enclosed note merely said 'From a wellwisher.' (We later found out that they came from a housebound old lady who saved all her small change for us). On the occasion of the snookerthon a little girl came in to watch, and sponsored one of the players for 10p. Little things that meant a lot.

I suppose that we were fortunate at the time of our Appeal, in that the National Lottery and the scratch card craze had not started, which could well have diluted the giving somewhat. On the other hand, we might have had a Meanwood millionaire helping us, or we might have been given a grant from the lottery funds. Who knows?

APPROACHING INDIVIDUALS. Although our data base of names and addresses was very useful, we decided early on that everyone in Meanwood should be contacted, and asked to help in some way. A letter was composed, and together with a leaflet and donation form, was delivered to every house in the district. Others to supporters further afield were obviously posted. I did offer to personally deliver the ones to America, Canada, Australia and New Zealand by hand, just for travelling expenses, but the rest of the Committee vetoed the idea!

We requested that donations be sent to the School, or they could be paid directly into the Meanwood branch of the Yorkshire Bank whichever was most convenient. We also explained the workings of the Covenanted Giving Scheme, and what a big advantage this would be to the Appeal, without costing the donor anything extra. Quite simply if a donor was a taxpayer, and signed a Covenant to pay to the Appeal a certain amount (at least £40 each year), for a minimum of four years, the Chancellor of the Exchequer would refund directly to us an additional third i.e. a gift of £60 would benefit the Appeal to the tune of £80. A number of individuals used this tax-efficient method to help us, and others used 'Give as You Earn' and 'Gift Aid' schemes. Legislation frequently changes in this area, and a watchful eye is needed to ensure maximum benefits are obtained.

We were delighted at the response to the letters, and donations were soon flowing in a few days after delivery.

In addition to this blanket approach I wrote many individual letters. These were to anyone who I considered might support our Appeal. For example, I sent one off to the man described in The Times as 'The highest paid man in Britain.' I must admit to being pleasantly surprised when I received a prompt reply and a cheque for £10! Every little helps.

I also popped off a missive to the Prime Minister, Margaret Thatcher, asking for a little help, and inviting her to visit the School. Shortly afterwards she was ousted from office, but I do not think the two were connected.

Many local readers will remember Doris Greenwell, the blind lady who in her later years lived in a flat on Green Road. She was a great enthusiast about anything to do with Meanwood, and the School Appeal in particular, and wrote about some of her schooldays memories in the 150th. Anniversary Brochure. She attended many of the early functions, and after her death, her two sons gave a very generous donation to the Appeal from her estate. They said it was a gesture of which they were sure she would have heartily approved. Very nice.

It is often said that it is not what you know, but WHO you know, and this was proved to be very true. Lord Grimthorpe, with his many personal contacts, was invaluable in this direction, and a number of sizeable donations were received as a direct result of his approaches to individuals, businesses, and charities. He also furnished us with names to approach ourselves.

Other Committee Members also contacted individuals known to them, and again proved the point that personal contacts win hands down over cold letters, which are virtually a waste of time and postage.

Do not think however that every contact guarantees a donation. We had quite a number of disappointments! Perseverance is the name of the game, and being on the lookout for snippets of information in the press, etc. often gives ideas as to who to try next.

Keep on trying. For example, when I saw that the comedy show 'Bread' was on at the Grand Theatre in Leeds I sent a little note to the star Jean Boht, and received by return a programme autographed by all the cast. This was sold off at one of the events. Similarly, all the cast of 'The Darling Buds Of May' gave me an autographed photograph that we put in the auction. Alan Bennett likewise sent us a copy of one of his books. Not all gifts are cash, but you can soon turn them into money.

'THE BIG ONE' came about by this steady process of writing to anyone with potential, and particularly where there was a Meanwood connection. Arthur Hopwood, in his book on the history of Meanwood, mentioned William Lawies Jackson who made his fortune in the last century in the tanning business, firstly at Meanwood Grove, and later at Buslingthorpe. He went on to become a Member of Parliament for 22 years, a Cabinet Minister, and later Lord Allerton of Allerton Hall. His son Sir Francis Stanley Jackson was a celebrated cricketer and Captain of Yorkshire. This seemed a promising lead when Arthur mentioned to me one day that there was a descendant living as a retired gentleman farmer in Leicester. He was George William Lawies Jackson,

10 DOWNING STREET

LONDON SW1A 2AA

From the Private Secretary

5 April 1990

Dear Mr Bewell,

Thank you for your letter of 3 March to the Prime Minister.

Mrs Thatcher was very interested to learn about the work of the Meanwood School building appeal and was impressed by how much you have managed to raise so far. As you will appreciate, the Prime Minister is asked to contribute to a great many voluntary causes and, although she likes to give as much support as she possibly can, she has had to make it a rule that she will only support causes and charities with which she has a close personal connection.

You asked whether she might visit you when she is next in your area. As I am sure you can imagine the Prime Minister is able to carry out far fewer visits of this kind than she would like because of the enormous pressures on her diary. However, I know she will want to bear the possibility of a visit to your village school in mind, should a suitable opportunity arise.

Yours sincerely,

CAROLINE SLOCOCK

Peter Bewell, Esq.

Reply to my letter to the Prime Minister

the Third Baron of Chapel Allerton, who was 87 years old, and had no surviving heirs.

I wrote a letter to him, and enclosed a copy of the Meanwood book for his general interest, and obviously told him all about the Appeal. There was no reply, and the reason became clear when I picked up the *Yorkshire Post* one morning and saw that he had died. The article also said he had left £1,397,348 Net, and went on to name the executors.

Off went a letter to the executors asking if there was any possibility that they would consider our Appeal in view of the family connections. Nothing ventured . . .

I wasn't too surprised that I heard nothing, but then on one memorable evening some months later (December 19th.1991 to be precise) we had just returned dog- tired from a M.S.B.A. carol singing outing at Leeds City Station when the phone rang. It was the Executor!

He wanted to know all that we were doing to raise funds, how much was still needed, what stage the new building work had reached, and we chatted for a long time generally. At the time we still needed about £59,000 to reach our target, and I obviously realised we were in with a chance of a donation, otherwise why was he ringing? You could have knocked me down with a feather, though, when he calmly said 'Well Mr Bewell, I have good news for you. You will not need to raise £59,000, only £49,000, as I am arranging for £10,000 to be sent to you during the next couple of weeks or so out of Lord Allerton's estate.' I thanked him profusely, wished him a Happy Christmas and put down the phone.

I immediately picked it up again, and rang the Vicar, the Headteacher, and as many of the Committee as I could contact, to give them the fantastic news and to invite them round the following evening to celebrate. What wonderful timing just before Christmas, especially as it would mean we had passed the magical £100,000 mark, and could announce the fact to the community at the Christmas services and celebrations.

It was a very exciting evening, but when I got to bed I started thinking it over, and doubts began to creep into my mind. Had he really said £10,000, or had my old ears deceived me, and he had said £1.000? Had I told everyone the wrong figure? It was a very long couple of weeks before the cheque eventually arrived, but thankfully it was for £10,000 and I could sleep again! What a boost for the funds, and what a tonic for all the workers and supporters.

The new School Hall now bears a plaque inscribed 'THE WILLIAM LAWIES JACKSON HALL.'

Now down to earth again. I had the bright idea (?) one day of tracking down all the places in the world called Meanwood and soliciting their help. After scouring the Library, I couldn't find one. Back to the drawing board, and see if there were any places called Leeds. Success! I found a number in Canada and the U.S.A. and promptly sent them all an appeal letter.

Not a penny (or a cent) did I receive! I did however get a number of replies, such as the one from Leeds in New York State that said how interesting, as they too were raising funds! In their case to dredge Leeds Pond. I also received a reply from Leeds in Ontario offering to sell me a book about their Leeds for $17.95! Oh well, it seemed like a good idea at the time.

During our 150th. Anniversary year I noticed that Kew Gardens were also celebrating the same anniversary, so I sent off a congratulatory letter, and the leaflets, etc., but alas, all I got in return was a £1 voucher. In the same year I noticed that Eton College had reached their 550th. anniversary, so off went a letter to their Bursar telling him the tale, and also drawing his attention to the fact that one of their former pupils had been Captain Oates of Antarctic fame, and how he had been connected to Meanwood. No luck there either, as they thought the connection too distant.

Despite the failures though, the overall exercise was well worth all the effort, and many hundreds of donations were received, varying from the old lady's coppers to the 'Big one'. All important in their own way.

DEDICATED GIVING SCHEME. Part way through the campaign we launched this scheme, which was an elaboration of the old 'Buy a Brick' idea. On reflection we should have started it right at the beginning.

We decided to put on offer various parts of the new building for people or organisations to sponsor, or 'Dedicate' as we termed it. There had to be a wide range of values so as not to preclude anyone, and we finished up with the following list of items and values;

Stones at £5 each. These proved very popular, and many people bought one or more. Some in their own name, and others in memory of a loved one. The only problem was when one lady wanted to know exactly which stone was hers, and would it have her name carved opon it? Tact and diplomacy were needed to carry the day!

Doors at £100 each. Quite a number of these were taken.

Windows at £500 each. Several were dedicated.

Practical areas at £1,000 each. Several of these were also received.

A *'Book of Dedications'* was written up towards the end of the Appeal, and recorded the names of all those who had contributed in any way. We also

Meanwood Church of England (Aided) Primary School

A CHANCE TO SHARE

THE NEXT 150 YEARS

WHAT NOW?

March 1992:

The long awaited building work commenced on 2nd March, with the Shepherd Construction Group Limited as main contractors.

The work is expected to take 14 months, so the new school should be opened in the **late Spring** of 1993 to welcome back the Staff and Children, who are being accomodated in Bentley Primary School whilst building is taking place.

****

If YOU will help us…

Please complete this simple form and return it, together with your donation, to:

Mr. G.B. Holland, Treasurer,
Meanwood School Building Appeal,
Yorkshire Bank Plc,
7, Capitol Parade,
Meanwood, Leeds LS6 4JA.

If you are a tax-payer donating over £40, **WE** can benefit if you **COVENANT** your gift. Please ask for details.

****

All enquiries to be addressed to:-

Mrs Cathy Stevens,
5 Quarry Gardens, Alwoodley, Leeds LS17 7NQ.
Tel: (0532) - 674769

Charity Registration Number 249860

Book of Dedication

The Faith To Build

YES! I have the faith to build a future, and would like the name................., to be inscribed in the Book of Dedication at Meanwood School.

I would like my bit of the future to be one or

more	*stones:*	£5 each ☐
	doors:	£100 each ☐
or,	a *window*;	£500 ☐
or,	a *Practical Area:*	£1000 ☐

(Please tick)

YES! I would like a part of the building to be named after.............., *and to bear a plaque recording the gift of -*

£3000: a *Courtyard* ☐
£5000: a *Classroom* ☐
£7500: the *Library* ☐

(Please tick)

Name:
Address:

Tel No:

☐ I wish to make a donation of £...........
☐ My gift is £40 or over. I should like details of covenanting.

(Please tick)

The Dedicated Giving Leaflet

THE FAITH TO BUILD A FUTURE

THEY shared the first 150 years....

Meanwood Church of England (Aided) Primary School is a Victorian gem in an idyllic rural setting, only minutes from one of the busiest city centres in the North of England. Its unusual belfry, its Schoolmaster's House, and the classroom provision, which grew to meet expanding needs over a period of 70 years from its foundation in 1840, give it an architectural distinction to merit its Grade II listing.

MANY, MANY PEOPLE have had the faith to build the future in Meanwood School's first 150 years.

THE BECKETT FAMILY's generosity and care for our village founded both school and church. Their concern continues to this day.

GENERATIONS OF CHILDREN have begun their schooling here, taking pride in this shared achievement. Many have grown up to send their children and grandchildren to the same enriching start to school life.

OUR MEANWOOD FRIENDS - church and chapel, business people, private individuals and local residents have joined parents and teachers in weaving the school into the very fabric of the village community, where it now serves as focus and unifying point for our village spirit.

Our enlarged and modernised school will cost approximately £1 million. As with all Church (Aided) school building projects, 85% of this will be provided by the Government, but the remaining 15%, or £150,000, has to be raised by the School Governors.

In just under three years, the Meanwood School Building Appeal WITH YOUR HELP has raised over £121,000. We now urgently need your help to raise the remaining £29,000.

...."one of the most remarkable and high quality school buildings in the city. A system of courtyards links together new and old in a most subtle and imaginative manner. This is a classic example of how the desire to retain the heritage of an area can be combined with the needs of the future."

Leeds Civic Trust Newsletter, October 1990.

YOU can share the next 150 years....

In September 1991, we opened a Book of Dedication to record donations. Friends of the School with the faith to build a future can dedicate in their own names, or in the name of a loved one, a part of the new building.

Stones may be dedicated for
donations of: £5 each

Doors: £100 each
Windows: £500 each
Practical Areas: £1000 each

For larger donations, the name of an individual, a Company or a Charitable Trust may be inscribed on a plaque to be displayed in the chosen part of the building:-

* **Community/Parent's Room:**   £2000
Courtyard: £3000
Classroom: £5000
Library: £7500
* **Hall:**   £10000

* *These have already been dedicated*

The Dedicated Giving Leaflet

incorporated into the book a list of all the events that had taken place, and the names of officials and Committee members.

The book was shown at the official opening, and other times, and there was always a queue of people eager to find their name in it. I admit to being worried on those occasions in case we had somehow missed out someone. We had a few hairy moments when the name couldn't be found first time but we were never caught out. The problems were usually when someone was looking for their own name, and had forgotten that they had put, say, Grandma's name, or their maiden name, on the dedication form. A local lady, Hazel Hunter wrote up the pages in lovely calligraphy, and they were then professionally bound in leather to make a book that will be kept in school for future generations to gaze upon.

APPROACHING CHARITIES. There are thousands of Charities and Charitable Trusts throughout the country, albeit the vast majority of them in London or the South East. Each is administered by Trustees, who are legally responsible for the investment of the Trust Funds, and their distribution. There were untold millions just waiting for our request, or so we thought!

In reality it wasn't quite like that though. Despite the fact that a Trust's purpose in life is to give money away to good causes, there is a stumbling block. Each Trust is controlled by a legally constituted Deed, and within that, there is a clause called 'The Objects', which clearly defines the type of good cause the originators wished to support. Quite often this also defines a 'Beneficial Area.' For example, it may be laid down that the 'Object' is for 'The relief of the poor and needy children of textile workers in the Parish of Batley.' No matter how good your cause might be, if it does not fall precisely into that description you will not get a penny, so don't bother writing!

It was therefore important for us to try to identify Trusts whose 'Objects' would allow them to make a grant to M.S.B.A. There are a number of Directories which give details of this nature, and although expensive, are worth obtaining. The main one is 'The Directory of Grant-making Trusts' that lists details of about 2,500 Trusts. It can be obtained from The Directory of Social Change. (See appendices).

There are a number of Regional offices such as the 'West Yorkshire Charities Information Bureau' in Wakefield that we found to be most helpful.

There are also innumerable other Trusts who choose not to be listed, and are quietly administered by Trustees who are often local solicitors. If you can track them down, fine.

Our Charities Sub-Committee trawled through these lists, and wrote to the ones they felt may be able to help most. They also asked our Patrons to help by speaking to any Trustees they knew.

It soon became evident that where there was not some form of personal contact the returns were few and far between. Where contact was established, however, there were a number of donations forthcoming. Several came from contacts of Lord Grimthorpe, and a number from Committee members who were involved in organisations such as the Oddfellows Lodge, and the West Riding Masonic Charities.

Another idea that we tried was to contact all the other 'Holy Trinity' Churches in the country, and ask for some brotherly assistance. These requests were met with a mixed response. One Church sent us £200, but the best we managed from the others was the odd five or ten pounds. Many did not reply, but the ones who did often seemed in a worse plight than we were. One Vicar said his Church was in dire straits and could not help, but enclosed a small personal donation.

Overall we were disappointed in the response from charities in general, but even so we banked several thousand pounds which were very welcome. In retrospect maybe we didn't quite get the approaches right?

Some of the big television appeals such as 'Children in Need' raise vast sums from the public, then have to give it all away, so don't be afraid to approach them if your charity fits the bill.

Although not Charitable Trusts, do not lose sight of many other sources of finance from Local Authorities, Central Government, and the E.C. Keep in close contact with your Local Councillors, M.P. and M.E.P.

APPROACHING INDUSTRY/COMMERCE. The Sub-Committee for this sector started in a similar way, by drawing up lists of potential donors, based upon their own knowledge of different industries, and businesses, such as my own in the construction sector. A lot of valuable contacts once again originated from Lord Grimthorpe, and also a number from Alan Pedley.

After considerable discussions a number of standard letters were drafted, and these were sent off to the Bishop of Ripon and Lord Grimthorpe for signing, as it was thought their signatures would add a bit of weight to them. They were sent off in batches, with say one month to all the construction sector, and the next month to computer companies, and so on.

I knew from my own business experience that nowadays companies are inundated with requests for help from all manner of good causes, including schools from far and near, and to stand any chance of success there had to be some form of link. This generally took the form of one of us knowing a Director, or at least a senior member of staff. Without such a connection it proved yet again that cold letters are a waste of time and postage.

The best method to pursue the personal contact was undoubtedly to 'Get on your bike' and go and see them. If that was impractical, a personal chat on the phone, or a very personal letter. Again it was not what you knew . . .

We did have moderate success from these known contacts, although not in every case by any means, but at the end of the day we received over £6,500. Well below my forecast, but taking into account the awful state of the economy at the time, it was very understandable, and certainly very welcome.

There were benefits other than cash, however, as some companies gave us items for raffles and sales, particularly the local traders, for which we were very grateful. There were also the companies who sponsored events such as The Leeds and Holbeck Building Society who did the Fun Run, and Minova Ltd., who twice sponsored the performances of The Messiah.

In some cases we managed to persuade companies to covenant their gifts, either with a lump sum deposited covenant, or the normal four annual payments. In other cases money was received from Trusts that had been set up by companies for charitable giving, and some used the Gift Aid Scheme.

Unfortunately (or otherwise) there are no large companies operating in Meanwood, but we were always on the lookout for likely donors by keeping an eye on the press. An example was when I read that ASDA were celebrating 25 years in business. Off went another letter congratulating them, and back came a letter of thanks and a cheque for £25.

The Yorkshire Bank was particularly good to us by looking after our financial matters, as well as donating through one of their Trusts. They also helped by allowing us to put up posters in the bank, and have collection jars on the counters, as well as acting as a donation receipt centre. The Leeds and Holbeck also allowed us to mount a window display in the Meanwood Branch early on in the campaign, which helped us with our early publicity.

Perhaps next time round we should have an appeal in an economic boom!

8
SPONSORSHIP

Sponsorship is an excellent method of fundraising. There are two kinds, the first being where a Company or individual sponsors a complete event, i.e. they pay all the costs. The second type is where individuals participate in an event, and get people to sponsor them for doing so. In some cases, such as the Fun Run, it was a combination of the two. Let us look in a bit more detail;

SPONSORSHIP OF EVENTS. We were fortunate in having several such events where all the costs were covered. This obviously makes a big difference to the net profit.

The biggest of these was the 'FUN RUN', a 4.5 mile run (or walk, stagger or crawl)! around Meanwood and Weetwood.

We had heard that the Leeds and Holbeck Building Society had been involved in sponsored runs before, so we approached the local branch, who in turn put us in touch with the right man in head office. He readily agreed to put one on for us. Wonderful!

Peter Smithson, one of the Committee, Nick Scott and some of their friends, had been involved previously in a similar event. They liaised with the Building Society for us, and on the day of the event, organised all the thousand and one things that had to be done.

The Society produced all the paperwork, such as sponsorship forms, publicity material, etc., and on the day they even arrived with a caravan for the officials. They also provided the prizes for the winners. A certificate and a medal were presented to everyone who finished the course.

The local supermarket gave us the free use of their carpark for the start and finish, refreshment stalls, etc. (This was before Sunday trading started.) The police supervised traffic control for the main road crossing, so all that remained for us to do was to provide a number of marshals to man the route and generally help with registrations and the like, plus of course encouraging as many people as possible to participate, and raise their own sponsorship money.

The Sponsored Run Poster

Gary Schofield, the England and Leeds Rugby League star, came along to officially start the race, and later presented the winners with their medals. His presence no doubt swelled the numbers of participants, particularly amongst the youngsters.

The race took place on a rather wet and dismal Sunday morning, and brollies were much in evidence among the spectators, and even carried by some of the runners. The runners ranged from some serious road racers to idiots like myself who plodded around as fast as their old legs and bellows permitted, and those who gallantly walked the course. Some were seen pushing prams, others carrying toddlers, and at least one dragged his dog along. (I'm not sure whether it was sponsored or not!)

Fancy dress was encouraged, and proved very popular. I dressed from head to toe in scarlet, and entered as the 'Scarlet Runner.' (There were various rude remarks about me being a 'has-bean'!) Anyway, I managed to get round in 40 minutes, being 88th out of 312 entrants, so I was quite pleased. Another runner disguised as a rabbit carried a bucket and collected coins on her way round.

Income was generated by entry fees, and by individuals obtaining sponsorship. A number of us had been standing outside the supermarket in fancy dress for a few days prior to the event, and this gained a lot of publicity, as well as several hundred pounds in sponsorships.

All the sponsorship monies were paid into the local branch of the Society by individuals, and some time later one of the Society's Managers came along to one of the Committee meetings and presented us with a cheque. This was a monster in two ways; firstly it measured about 4 feet by 2 feet, and secondly it was for £2,315! An excellent affair, and one where a lot of people had a lot of fun, and well worth a few aching muscles next morning.

We tried to repeat the event the following year, but alas, when we approached the Society there had been a change of policy, and they were no longer sponsoring such events. We were very grateful to them however for helping to boost our funds to such a large extent.

Another very good Company sponsored event was the performance of HANDEL'S MESSIAH in Meanwood Parish Church, by The St. Peter's Singers, under the leadership of Simon Lindley. All the costs were paid for by a Morley textile company, MINOVA Ltd. where I had a good contact, and the net result was that all the admission monies, amounting to £712, became profit. In addition we made a fair amount from sales and donations on the night.

MINOVA very generously repeated their sponsorship the following Christmas that raised another £709.

A third such event was a performance in the Methodist Chapel by the YORKSHIRE POST BRASS BAND. A very popular concert, where this time all the costs were covered by an individual. The result was another £465 into the kitty, plus again some sales and donations on the night.

SPONSORSHIP OF INDIVIDUALS. This is where people engage in an activity that they like doing anyway, such as swimming, walking, running, riding, etc., and persuading their relations, friends, neighbours, and Uncle Tom Cobleigh and all, to pay them for doing it! I personally feel it is a bit like begging, with the participants getting all the fun, and the poor old donors getting only holes in their wallets, but there is no doubt about it being an extremely effective method of raising funds. A healthy one too, and generally the activities are ones that the children as well as older people can join in with. It is quite surprising how many miles a pre-school toddler can cheerfully (sometimes) clock up, as many a sponsor has discovered to their cost!

The amount promised can either be in the form of a lump sum for participating in the event, or can be an amount based upon achievement, such as per length, per mile, per hour, etc. From a fundraiser's point of view the latter is much more rewarding, as little Johnny whom the sponsor thought would walk a couple of miles, will probably churn out ten without batting an eyelid, and to his great delight will be very soon knocking on the door demanding his dues. The prudent sponsor may well be advised to plump for the fixed sum method!

Good organisation is essential, particularly from the safety angle, and things like road crossing marshals, back-up vehicles, and first-aiders on walks and runs are very important, as are attendants and lifesavers on swims. Close liaison with the police is also advisable.

We had quite a number of such events during the Appeal period, and without fail they all proved superb money raisers. Care has to be taken however to prevent 'Sponsor fatigue', so don't have too many in any one year.

SWIMMING. Bev Simpson and her team led this one, which turned out to be the most profitable of all. The Manager of the local authority pool at Kirkstall generously agreed to let us have the free and exclusive use of a number of lanes in the pool for two hours per night for a week. Quite a number of the children, parents, and staff went along on one or more evenings and swam their hearts out for M.S.B.A. A healthy activity, as well as bringing in the incredible amount of £1,715. Helpers were on hand to count and certify the number of lengths covered, so that the swimmers could prove to their sponsors what incredible distances they had swum! On a number of occasions children had to be virtually pulled out of the water, otherwise they would still be swimming away today! Cathy tells the story about her daughter Eleanor, who at the time of the first swim, always apparently swam as if she was about to drown. A very concerned attendant ordered her out after ten lengths, much to her disgust. The following year however she swam a mile, and took great delight in telling the same attendant in no uncertain manner!

No doubt, this was the best 'profit to effort ratio' from the organisers' point of view, and was repeated the following year with similar results.

FAMILY WALKS. We had two of these. The first one was a delightful 12 mile walk around what is known as the Cavendish Circuit. It starts and finishes near Bolton Abbey in Wharfedale, and traverses some lovely countryside, as well as going over the top of Simon's Seat. We were lucky with the weather, as it was an ideal sunny day, and 21 of us thoroughly enjoyed the excursion. Unfortunately the 22nd. did not.

Joyce Kirk, a middle-aged lady from the Church, slipped on some loose stones on the descent of Simon's Seat, and finished up being carried down the rest of the way by Peter Smithson and Alan Corners. I reckon it was about a mile, but Peter and Alan swear it was ten! Barbara Blakeney was waiting with a back-up car at the bottom, and after rendering first aid she took Joyce to Otley Hospital. She was later transferred to Leeds where a broken ankle was confirmed, and she eventually arrived home some days later with a pot leg. Ever game for a good cause though, Joyce turned the situation to advantage by charging for the 'Privilege' of autographing her pot, as I found out to my cost when visiting her in the Infirmary!

All the walkers, including Joyce, received a certificate, and M.S.B.A. was better off by £796.

The second walk was the 'Wharfedale Wander', a 7 mile ramble around the beautiful Burnsall area. Sixty six brave souls turned out for this one, and £850 was raised.

Both the walks were checked out by the organiser, Peter Smithson, beforehand, and transport, first aid, refreshments, etc. were laid on for the day. It certainly paid off when the accident occurred.

SNOOKERTHON. What on earth is one of these?

Well, it was a term coined by the members of the Meanwood Trinity Men's Society when they came up with the bright idea of getting a number of volunteers(?) to give up a good night's sleep to play snooker non-stop for twenty-four hours.

Ten idiots, including myself, duly turned up at The Meanwood Institute in Green Road one Friday evening, resplendent in fancy waistcoats and bow ties.

At seven o'clock precisely play commenced on the two tables. This meant that eight of us were playing, and two 'resting' at any one time. The sitting out periods always seemed extremely short, and certainly not long enough to have a decent nap, although a newspaper photographer managed to get a good shot of Pete Spedding having one!

Lots of supporters kept popping in to wish us well and encourage us throughout the whole period, and the collection jars did well, in addition to getting more sponsors as things went along. The early hours of Saturday morning seemed to be the worst, tending to drag, but even then we had visitors, some of whom brought welcome tasty morsels to keep us going.

All the players had obtained good sponsorship, in addition to which, some of the non-playing members had stood outside the supermarket in the cold and rain publicising the event, and getting more sponsors.

All in all it was a very jolly occasion, and, despite the weariness, we all thoroughly enjoyed the experience. When all the money was collected in we were able to give M.S.B.A. a cheque for £807. The quality of the snooker however was a different story, and when I tell you that a competition for the highest break in the tournament, was won by Alan Corners with a break of 25, you will realise that those lads at the Crucible have little to fear. It was high enough for Alan to take home the prize of a bottle of whisky though.

A DOGWALK. Another seemingly daft idea from Cathy made £360 for the funds. Nineteen dog lovers took part, together with their dogs, whose pedigrees ranged from 'posh' to what can only be politely described as 'dubious.' They all tramped happily around the park and woodlands (as they did most days anyway) and believe it or not, sponsors paid them for doing it. That's how daft (but very effective) sponsorship is. It just proves again how you can make money out of the most unlikely ideas.

AEROBICS. To be honest I am not quite sure how this one worked, and I certainly didn't participate. I do know though that a group of enthusiastic ladies meeting in the Parochial Hall sent £223 for the Appeal. Well done ladies.

SILENCE. It seems quite remarkable, but true, that a room full of youngsters can be quiet for a long period. It took place in School, and at so much per minute, it added up to a tidy sum, as some sponsors can vouch for! Harassed parents might like to try this at home sometime.

SLIMMING. Geoff Holland, our Treasurer, was told by his doctor that he should lose some weight, so he turned the situation to the advantage of

M.S.B.A. and got himself sponsored by the bank staff and various unwary customers like myself, at so much per pound lost. Another winner for us, but whether he has retained his weight at that level is another question.

RUNNING AND RIDING. Two parents had the novel idea of cycling from Liverpool to Leeds which raised funds, and several others ran in marathons and half marathons for us. One parent even ran the London Marathon bringing in a substantial amount. All excellent solo efforts.

****

Having the good ideas in the first place is of course the main essential, but the organisation of the event is so important if you are to get the maximum advantage out of it. Do not waste any opportunities.

Participants have to be recruited by fair means or foul, and sponsorship forms distributed in good time before the event. These can be given to all supporters, not just those taking part.

When the event is over, the task of getting all the promised monies in is not easy, and has to be pursued with vigour at times. At best it takes a few weeks to finally settle up. At the end of an event we would usually ask people how much they reckon they would be getting, so that we had some idea of what to expect. When the final totals were calculated we were more often than not pleasantly surprised, as it was in excess of the original figures. Care must be taken in accounting for every sponsorship form distributed, and meticulous records maintained. A letter of thanks was sent to all those who took part in the sponsored events, but it was impossible to thank all the thousands of people who had sponsored them.

People collecting sponsorship should always carry the official forms to show that they are genuine. On one occasion we were told that three boys were going round local houses knocking on doors and saying they were collecting for M.S.B.A. after completing a bike ride. Luckily we managed to track them down and nipped it in the bud. A tactful visit to the parents stopped it, and resulted in a £6 donation to the funds. You have to be careful.

> *Love it, or hate it, sponsorship in its different forms cannot be ignored, and is a major weapon in the fundraiser's armoury.*
>
> *Keep looking for new ideas. Even the daft ones!*

9
RAFFLES

These fall into two categories: The major ones sold to the public in general over several weeks, and the smaller type which are sold at a function and drawn the same day. Let us consider the major ones first.

For the first one we had to consider how many tickets to have printed, and we decided to go for 20,000. Although we didn't sell them all, it proved about right, and enabled us to have a large network of sellers. The tickets, priced at 20p. each, were bound in books of five. The vast majority were sold in this form at the convenient figure of £1, although some were sold singly. Under the terms of the licence each ticket had to show certain information such as the lottery registration number, price, main prizes, date and place of the draw, and the name and address of the promoter (myself). The promoter has to be responsible to the licence-issuing authority for the general fair conduct of the lottery, and when it is over, submit a full set of accounts showing all costs, sales, details of unsold tickets, and the net result.

We held three, and the net return was just over £2,000 each, which is obviously a major item in any fundraiser's language. For this type of lottery it is necessary to obtain a licence. (See Administration chapter).

In order to produce the accounts it was essential to have a first-class system of recording where every single ticket was allocated, and ensuring cash, stubs, and any unsold tickets were returned to the organiser prior to the draw. There was a lot of work in doing all this, and chasing up the late ones, but Cathy made an excellent job of it all. Her accounts were only wrong once, and that was when she had two pounds too much on one occasion! As promoter all I had to do, apart from doing my share of selling, was to sign the accounts at the end. Two checkers were also required to sign, and our auditor vetted the whole proceedings.

The basic distribution system was organised by giving each of the Committee members, parents of children in school, and as many other supporters as we could persuade, twenty books to sell. The majority sold them, and many came back for more. The best ones sold several hundred books. Another method of selling was outside the local supermarket. They gave us permission to set up a stall on certain days just prior to the draw and we manned the stall in pairs, on a rota basis. My turn usually coincided with the wet, cold, and windy days, or so it seemed, but it was another interesting experience, and a fascinating place to observe human nature, and have a chat with all and sundry. Quite a social occasion really. There were those who upon seeing us would lower their eyes and pretend not to notice, or in some cases even cross the road to avoid having to buy a ticket. Others would say 'Sorry I have no change, I will buy some on the way out.' Some honoured the promise, but not all. Some mumbled something incoherent, and hurried about their business, but in the main when people saw what it was for, they were very generous and some just gave a donation without taking any tickets. (This had to be kept in a separate jar to avoid fouling up the accounts). Some days we sold over £200 worth of tickets.

Each raffle had between 20 and 30 prizes. Most of these originated from redeeming the petrol coupons which had been collected (see chapter on collecting), and others were of gifts from businesses and individuals. To catch the punter's eye however, there always had to be a big attractive prize such as a 'Weekend in Paris for Two' or a television set, and these were purchased. One of the draws we entitled 'Sports and Leisure Draw' and we managed to compile an attractive prize list, such as a football signed by the Leeds United players, a cricket bat signed by the Yorkshire team, a Leeds Rugby League shirt, a rugby ball signed by the Great Britain side, and no end of general sports goods, generously donated when I went round all the sports shops in Leeds. We were also given free cinema and theatre tickets. The only complaint was that the prizes were too male-oriented, but we still sold as many tickets as the other raffles.

The draw was always made at one of the main social events, as this had a twofold effect. One, it sold more tickets for the event, and secondly, we sold quite a number of raffle tickets in the last couple of hours before the draw.

In the case of the small raffles we held one at nearly every event throughout the whole Appeal, and overall they must have made a significant contribution to the funds. By soliciting friends and local businesses we were nearly always able to produce a good range of prizes at no cost. On one occasion I recall a lovely knitted rabbit, complete with a Meanwood School uniform, being made, and given as a prize by a local lady. It was won by Anne Burgess, the deputy headteacher, and it is now used as the netball team trophy. The tickets were sold at most events right from the opening time, and the draw would take place fairly late on, so as to ensure as many sales as possible.

A FEW TIPS.

In small raffles, use the type of cloakroom tickets that have five to a page as most people will buy a full strip of five. Price the tickets modestly, say 10p or 20p.each.

Display the prizes and tempt the punters.

Have a reasonable number of prizes rather than one big one. That way more people go home happy!

When the winners come up to claim their prizes check the number and colour carefully.

Remember that young persons under 16 years old are not permitted to sell or purchase lottery tickets.

Do not give alcoholic prizes to under 18's.

When organising larger raffles have as large a sales force as possible, and encourage them to sell outside the normal area i.e. at their place of work, or their sports clubs, etc., and to distant friends and relatives.

Sellers must ensure that the purchaser's name, and at least a telephone number, are written on the back of **every** stub.

In the case of the major raffles, make sure the books of tickets are ordered in good time from a printer who is used to this type of work, and start selling three months before the draw.

Meticulously record the whereabouts of every ticket at all times.

At the time of the draw, carefully record the numbers as they are drawn, and have a second person checking each one before announcing them. Then write the numbers on a large blackboard. Bearing in mind in the case of the big raffles that a lot of the winners may not be present in the Hall at the time of the draw, display the winners' list as soon as possible on notice boards around the area, particularly where the main sales have taken place, such as the supermarket. Also have a printed list available to give to anyone on request.

Distribute the prizes as quickly as possible.

Strictly speaking when selling to the public, such as outside the supermarket, selling should be passive. That is, you should not 'buttonhole' people and pressure them into buying, but let them approach you.

Happy gambling!

10

SALES

We had a wide variety of goods for sale throughout the Appeal. Jackie Brewer headed up the small Sub-Committee to co-ordinate everything, and was assisted by Barbara Blakeney and Bev Simpson. She was a real force to be reckoned with, and not many people in Meanwood escaped her sales patter. Her husband Alan also worked hard transporting goods around venues, as well as tolerating the house being transformed into a shop for nearly four years!

Jackie operated stalls at all the events, both indoor and outdoor, as well as at any other place where the opportunity presented itself. A permanent stall was arranged at the back of the Church, and at various times in the Methodist schoolroom, outside the Supermarket, in School, and at Ivy Cottage. Opportunism was the name of the game and I don't think many chances were missed.

In addition to the main stalls, some of the children contributed by making and selling things, such as the numerous plaster models that Ben Thwaites and Nicholas Mohammed churned out. They made £138. The children of class four wrote and produced a little newspaper that made another £40, and several other children sold toys.

Other people made, and sold things themselves, and gave the proceeds to M.S.B.A. Peggy and Frank Ashton excelled at this and produced all manner of goods ranging from marmalade to carved wooden Yorkshire roses, from which they contributed a considerable sum to the funds.

Many other goods were made or gathered, and sold privately or given to Jackie to sell. These included lots of knitted articles made by Mums and Grans, fruit in season, homemade jams, marmalade, plants, garden produce, dried flower arrangements, Christmas tree decorations, lavender bags, dolls, etc. In other cases we bought items in bulk, such as garden bulbs that the Headteacher Bryn Evans hauled from Lincolnshire each year, and toiletries which we bought at a factory in Derbyshire. Other bulk buys included biscuits, chocolate, and a large quantity of end-of-the-line Adidas sports clothing.

Wooden items were always a good seller, particularly for Christmas gifts, and we had a number of good supporters who produced excellently-crafted items for us to sell. Jim Durrant's superb wood turnings were always in great demand, and we even had a waiting list at one period. My contribution in this direction was to churn out innumerable bird tables, bird houses, and nesting boxes for small birds, plus a special order for some owl and bat boxes. These were generally sold to the passing public from Ivy Cottage, and I still get people knocking on the door asking for them, but alas, stocks are exhausted and they are unlucky. Other good sellers were the souvenirs I made from some old 5" by 4" pine beams salvaged from the school. I cut these into 1" slices, fixed on a nice gold label which read 'This is a genuine piece of the old Meanwood C.of E. School 1840-1990' and sold hundreds at 50 p. a time. Goodness knows what people did with them!

At the time I was selling these wooden slices, David Jason and Pam Ferris, who were filming in the school, kindly autographed some of them for me. David asked me how much I was going to sell them for, and I tentatively suggested that with his signature on them I could double the price to a pound. Not likely, he said, don't take less than a fiver apiece! He was right, I sold them all at that figure in no time at all.

The Vicar, Richard Wiggen, requested a moveable rack for the Church, in which to place the flags of the uniformed organisations on parade services. Using salvaged timbers from the school I made one for him and received a nice donation for M.S.B.A. The rack now resides at the rear of the church, and it carries the little gold 'genuine' label of course. I was honoured to think that a little bit of my work, complete with my ivy leaf trademark, was placed in a church which has so much wonderful work by the famous woodcarver Robert Thompson, who is known worldwide as 'The Mouseman of Kilburn' because of the little mouse which is carved somewhere on every piece. (Next time you visit the church see how many you can find).

One amusing event occurred when we tried to sell an old, dirty, cast iron door stop in the shape of a cat, which had propped open the school entrance door since the year dot. Nobody seemed interested at all until Owen Hogg the School caretaker came along and suggested we gave it a name. How about calling it 'Oggy's Moggy' he said. We did so, and got a fiver for it in five minutes!

The history book 'Meanwood' that had been written by Fred Casperson and Arthur Hopwood had been on the market for a few years and was still selling steadily. Arthur said the present stocks were almost exhausted, and would M.S.B.A. consider paying for another reprint of a thousand copies costing just over a thousand pounds. If so, the Authors would donate the whole of the proceeds to the Appeal. The Committee considered the offer, accepted with thanks, and proceeded. A decision well vindicated, as they sold very well at the events, and at a special promotion at the supermarket. I also cashed in on the general election in 1992 by having a bookstall outside the entrance to the local polling station. (I'm not quite sure if it was 'legal' but it worked!) There are still a few copies left. (See appendices.)

On one occasion, just before the old school was handed over to the builders, we held a silent auction of some old furniture and bits and pieces. A strict time limit was set for two hours after the opening, and each item in the sale had a piece of paper attached, on which prospective buyers could write an offer. Others could then see what had been offered and better it if they wished. It was a real cat and mouse affair that became more exciting as the time drew near for the final bell, with eager and hopeful buyers dashing around to see if theirs was still the best offer, and if not, perhaps upping it again. At the end there were some very happy buyers, but others were disappointed. Our Treasurer was certainly happy.

On the same day we sold, in an ordinary fashion, all sorts of bits and pieces, such as old and musty maps and wall charts of the 'Great British Empire' which hadn't seen the light of day for many a long year. I also stripped out of the cloakrooms hundreds of Victorian coathooks, and after adding one of the magic gold labels they too sold like hot cakes. Other items included old fireguards that were relics from the days of open fires, old blackboards, and even some old roof slates. (All complete with the genuine labels of course).

Geoff Holland did a couple of excellent pen sketches for us. One was of the school from the Green Road side, and the other of the old bell tower from the courtyard. These were reproduced as notelets, and as large prints for framing, and proved very popular. The sketch of the school was also emblazoned on souvenir mugs, another good line. In total we sold several thousand copies in various forms, much to Geoff's delight.

We always tried to give value for money, and in quite a number of cases, such as the Meanwood book we had to 'speculate to accumulate'. We only came unstuck once, and that was when we had too many copies of the 150th. Anniversary Brochure printed. (If you know anybody who would like to buy, at a bargain price, a few hundred copies give me a ring, PLEASE!)

Another excellent selling line was the teatowels that we had printed. The first batch had four local views on them, The Church, Chapel, School, and Institute, and were very popular. They sold at £2.95 each and we made about a pound on each sale. An even better one came up. All the children in the school were given a piece of paper, and asked to draw themselves. These were then sent to the manufacturer who made them into a marvellous teatowel featuring every child. You can imagine what the sales of these were like, as every Mum. Grandma, and Aunt wanted a copy. I suspect many were kept as souvenirs rather than used for drying the pots, as they are very amusing to say the least. Needless to say we repeated the exercise in later years as new children joined the school. L.S.Lowry has nothing on some of the Meanwood matchstick men. One edition had a spelling mistake, with Meanwoood gaining another o, but surprisingly nobody noticed it until they had been on sale for several weeks. If misprinted teatowels were like misprinted stamps we would have been worth millions! I did suggest another printing, this time using drawings made by the Staff of themselves, but this was howled down.

A number of specialist 'Parties' were held, often in individuals' houses, selling such items as Tupperware, Lingerie, Allsorts, Fashions, Knickerbocker Glory and Jewellery. In these cases the Appeal benefited by receiving a percentage of the sales. Although I did not attend any of these, I understand they were often good fun, and it was only recently that I received a confession from one of the organisers. One of the events recorded in the accounts as a Tupperware party was in fact a 'Naughty Underwear Party', and they hadn't dared tell me at the time. (Maybe they thought I might gatecrash!) One of the Fashion Shows was held in the School, and all the models were lady volunteers. Apparently some were suffering from 'Catwalk Fright' until the organiser produced a 3 litre box of wine. I understand the rest of the show went extremely well, and if any agencies are looking for new models, just give me a ring, and I will put them in touch with some Meanwood talent.

One evening in the local paper there was a small advertisement saying that a local company had a quantity of soft toys that they were willing to give away to any worthwhile charities. Apply in person the next day at 10 a.m. I quickly re-arranged my schedule, and rolled up on their doorstep at the appointed hour and explained what M.S.B.A. was all about. They immediately agreed it was a worthwhile home for their toys and loaded up my car to the roof with boxes of brand new soft toys. It had come about because they had ordered them all for a big Christmas sales promotion, but they had not turned up in time. A case of one person's misfortune being another's gain. We sold the lot very quickly. Another example of keeping your eyes open and acting quickly.

During the first summer we had the bright idea of cashing in on the many visitors to Meanwood Park and the woods by selling cups of tea, coffee, glasses of juice, and sweets, crisps, etc. on Saturday and Sunday afternoons. We sited a stall adjacent to the school, and in the entrance to the Park and did quite well. A Tombola stall was also quite popular. Alas, we couldn't get enough volunteers to take turns at operating the stalls, and it lapsed after a few weeks, but not before we banked £199 profit. It was time consuming, and a bit of a trouble hauling the stall, gas boiler, gas bottle, water, and stock. It was a classic case of a poor return for the effort involved. That was one event we did not repeat the following year.

We had some aerial photographs of the School, and Meanwood in general, taken professionally, and these sold as straightforward prints, or were framed to order. They now grace many a wall in the district, as well as being sent all over the world to Meanwood exiles. My only disappointment was that they would not allow me to go on the photographer's flight due to insurance restrictions.

During the 150th. Anniversary celebrations children were encouraged to come to school one day in Victorian dress, and that created another making and selling opportunity, with enterprising Mums producing smocks, mob caps and the like.

Anything bearing the name Meanwood was a sure seller, and we produced mugs, sets of coasters, jockey caps, pens and badges. There are a number of specialist firms that produce these sorts of things.

Martin Cockerill, one of the Dads, videoed many of the activities and events, edited the footage, and produced some fine and interesting copies for sale. They went well, and will be cherished in the years to come. Les Mann also produced and sold some of his tapes.

Zurich had nothing on Meanwood when the School Secretary's husband, Alan Jones, started manufacturing the Meanwood version of gnomes, together with a variety of animals in concrete, donating a percentage of the sales to the Appeal. The evidence is now seen in many a local garden.

****

> *Never refuse an offer of anything to sell. Someone, somewhere, sometime, will buy it!*
>
> *Advertise for all you are worth. Tell the world what you have for sale, how much it costs, and where it can be bought.*
>
> *Always have good stocks of everything in the run-up to Christmas. That is when sales peak.*
>
> *Finally on the subject of sales . . . If it moves, sell it a ticket for something . . . if it doesn't move, put it on the stall and sell it.*
>
> *The best of luck!*

11
EVENTS IN GENERAL

Throughout the period of the Appeal we kept up a steady stream of events, both indoor and outdoor. The majority were arranged by ourselves, but others were fully organised by others, such as the Church, the Chapel, Meanwood Village Association, Parent's Association, Guides, and individuals.

A Social Sub-Committee was formed to co-ordinate events. Anne Burgess had the difficult task of chairing this Committee and was ably assisted by Cathy Stevens, Christine Holmes, Janet Thornton, Bev Simpson and Heather Booth. It was the hardest working Committee of all, with little respite throughout the whole period. They had to receive and vet all ideas which came forward, ensure an even flow of events, and arrange a good variety to suit all ages and tastes, as well as ensuring that dates didn't clash with other events in the neighbourhood. This latter point was a difficult problem and we slipped up once or twice before Anne Burgess started a 'Community Diary.'

We made a rule that every event had to have a person or Sub-Committee responsible for the whole affair, from planning through to reconciliation of the accounts. When an event was mooted at the Main Committee there was usually a deafening silence when I asked for a volunteer to run it, but in the end someone always did. The job of the 'Event Director' was to ensure that the many tasks needed to make the event a success were delegated to members of the Committee or others. With some experience, it soon became clear which people were good at which jobs. Horses for courses as they say.

As readers will see in the next chapter, the events ranged from little coffee mornings organised by individuals, through to complex events like the Auction and Car Boot sale organised by a Sub-Committee and where a lot of volunteers were needed. All were important in their own way in achieving our goal.

Where events were held at the Church, Chapel, School, Conservative Club, Institute or the Working Men's Club no room hire charges were levied, which helped considerably.

We found out by experience which type of events were the most popular and profitable, and repeated them after a decent interval. We also kept an eye on what we came to call the 'Profit to effort ratio.' There was no point in putting a lot of time and effort into something that say made £100, when perhaps for the same amount of effort, or maybe just a little bit more, we could have made £1,000 in a different direction.

In many cases the admission money was the main source of revenue, and it was important to pitch the price at the right level. As high as possible, but still sending the customers away happy, and asking 'When is the next one?' As I have said before 'Value for money' was at the top of our list.

Rather than just take admission money on the gate or door, we found it far better to sell tickets before the day. We soon built up a list of likely purchasers for the different types of events. Tickets were prepared and distributed around the Committee members some three weeks or so before the day, which gave ample time for sales. We found that the bulk of sales usually took place in the last few days before the event, and this sometimes caused a few anxious times wondering if it was going to be successful. Another thing we noticed was that about 10% of people who bought tickets never turned up on the day. We could only put this down to the fact that some were bought simply to help the Appeal, and the purchasers never intended coming anyway. Others no doubt were unable to come because of illness or some last minute hitch. It was very interesting to note that out of all the many thousands of tickets we sold over the three and a half years, only one man (who shall be nameless!) asked for his money back because he had been unable to attend an event. I was so surprised at his request I agreed!

We obviously required many thousands of tickets, and to avoid the problem and cost of having them printed for every single event, we had a large quantity printed with the basic information on, and then filled in the details by hand each time. Time consuming, but cost effective. Several basic colours were used to avoid any confusion.

Another lesson we learnt early on was that when you bring in outside caterers it makes a big hole in the profits, so whenever practical we did the catering ourselves. A similar situation existed with the bars. We found an excellent local supplier of pork pies which were always popular, and an off-licence shop where we had a sale or return arrangement. This did not apply of course to part-used bottles, so we steered clear of spirits and concentrated on a simple bar. Cathy was usually saddled with the job of doing the 'booze run' as she called it, and on one occasion her fully laden trolley decided (as they usually do) to go the way IT wanted, and tipped over. She stuck out her foot to stop it, and finished up hobbling around Meanwood for several weeks cursing M.S.B.A. and anyone in earshot! On another visit to the off-licence she had about £350 worth of drinks lined up at the check-out when the man behind remarked it looked like it was going to be a great party and could he come? 'Yes, if you buy a ticket' she replied!

> **TIPS.** Over the three and a half years, we obviously gained a lot of experience in what to do, and what not to do, to make an event a success.
> The following tips may help readers in organising their events. I hope so, as a lot of the experience was gained the hard way!
>
> **EVALUATE** any idea before proceeding, to ensure as far as practical that it will be a profitable event, and that the net profit will be commensurate with the effort.
>
> **APPOINT** an 'Event Director' to be responsible for everything.
>
> **PLAN** the event in good time, and ensure volunteers are forthcoming for all the necessary jobs.
>
> **ADVERTISE** by all possible means, such as posters, leaflets, press, radio, television, Church notices, etc., but most importantly, by word of mouth. Get out there, and tell the world what is taking place and SELL THE TICKETS. It is no good putting on the finest of events if no customers come through the door. These sales should take place in the two or three weeks prior to the event. On the morning of the big day put out some large notices around the area to remind people, and bring in some last minute sales. We often sold a lot of last minute tickets standing outside the supermarket on the morning of the event. Remember when catering that there will always be some who turn up at the door without tickets, so allow for a few extras.
>
> **REMOVE** all the notices as soon as the event is over. Nothing looks worse than seeing outdated notices around.
>
> **INFORM** any households adjacent to the event if there is any likelihood that it will inconvenience or disturb them. Far better to deal with the situation prior to the day, than have to deal with complaints later. We found everyone very understanding when dealt with in this way.
>
> **OBTAIN** any licences necessary. These often have to be applied for some weeks in advance.
>
> **AVOID** school holiday periods generally, as a lot of potential customers will be away.

CHECK that the venue is available, and book it firmly before advertising the event. Check the access and keys situation. Check if there are limits on numbers.

BOOK the Band, Choir, Speaker or whatever. Confirm immediately in writing, and then check on the phone a few days before the event.

SET a maximum number for ticket sales. (This may be laid down by the venue owner's fire certificate or licence.) It is also wise to have a minimum number of sales in mind, and if this is not reached, cancel the event rather than have a loss-making flop.

PRINT and number the tickets in good time and distribute them around the sales force two or three weeks in advance.

ORDER the catering requirements, and ensure things like crockery, cutlery, glasses, etc. are available at the venue. If not, arrange to hire them.

If a number of events are planned, it will pay you to purchase a quantity rather than hiring every time, and it will be more convenient. If you are buying your drinks from a wine merchant or decent sized shop you will find that they will probably have a scheme of free loans or low cost hiring of glasses. Please do not use plastic plates and glasses, as nothing puts people off more, (even though they save on the washing up). Remember the little things like table cloths, teacloths, serviettes, table decorations etc. Check there are sufficient tables and chairs.

BEG, borrow, or steal a good P.A. system, and most importantly make sure that there will be somebody there who knows how to set it up and use it efficiently.

VARY the venues, as each one will probably appeal to a different section of the community.

DON'T FORGET the bits and pieces such as the pepper and salt, washing up liquid, dishcloths, binbags, vinegar, sauces, and toilet rolls. (We were once 'caught short' on this last one, and someone had to make a quick dash to the supermarket!)

ARRANGE for the helpers to be there in good time to set it all up, and don't forget you will need them at the end to do all the clearing up.

MAKE, and display prominently, signs for things like bar prices, raffle details, what the next event is, and the latest total on the fund raising.

OBTAIN cash floats from the bank sufficient for all the stalls, bar, etc.

ORGANISE some extra little money-making by way of a raffle or game.

SET UP a sales stall if practical.

> **HAVE** *a large poster made, and displayed, showing where the profits are going, other ways that people can help, and some names, addresses and telephone numbers of officials for further information. Never give anyone an excuse to say they didn't know about your good cause.*
>
> **ANNOUNCE** *during the event how the appeal is going along, and give details about forthcoming events. Sell tickets for the next event if it is imminent.*
>
> **SELL OFF** *any surplus food at the end of the event. Make it cheap, as it is better to recoup some of the cost, rather than be left with a load of stale stuff that then is thrown away.*
>
> **LEAVE** *the venue as you found it (or better). This may mean bringing some new bin bags for disposing of the rubbish. Don't forget to pass the aluminium cans, and foil to the scrap collectors. If everything has to be cleared from the venue on the night of the event, make sure there are sufficient cars and sober drivers available to transport it.*
>
> **BANK** *the cash, or pop it in the nightsafe as soon as possible, and take a colleague along for security.*
>
> **RETURN** *the venue keys.*
>
> **RECONCILE** *the accounts whilst it is still fresh in the mind, and pay all the bills promptly.*
>
> **KEEP** *good records of everything, you will find them very valuable if the event is repeated, or for organising similar affairs.*
>
> **ENSURE** *that there is ample car parking, and if necessary arrange for an attendant, or several on a shift system.*

I am sure that any reader who has organised any events will be able to add to my list. Do so, record things whilst you remember them, and it will make life easier the next time you buckle down to sorting it all out.

Happy eventing!

12
SPECIAL EVENTS

THE LAUNCH

To officially launch the Appeal in June 1989 we had two open evenings in the old School. For the first one we invited all the parents, Church members, and known supporters, to come along and see and hear what it was all about. The second one, a few days later, was similar and was for the general public. There were displays of the architect's drawings, children's work, old photographs, newspaper cuttings and a general explanation about the whole project by the headteacher, Bryn Evans.

I explained the various means by which people could help, by contributing not only their cash, but devoting some time and using their talents. The newly printed leaflets and donation forms were distributed and advice was on hand for those who were considering covenanting, etc.

Lots of people turned up from far and wide. I am not sure of the numbers that came on the first evening, but on the second one over three hundred arrived. Nostalgia was very much in evidence, and this later proved to be an important factor in the whole campaign. Overall the two evenings were a great success, and we were well and truly on our way.

Fundraising was started even before the official launch, and the Meanwood Village Association jumped the gun with an evening of 'Meanwood Nostalgia' and a supper ten days beforehand.

150th ANNIVERSARY

'THAT WAS THE WEEK THAT WAS!'

The School was founded by Christopher Beckett in 1840, so we were fortunate that the time to celebrate the 150th. anniversary fell during the Appeal period.

We were unable to establish the exact date of the opening, so we decided that May would be a suitable time, and so it was.

A small sub-committee was formed to organise the festivities, and they quickly made two important decisions. The first was that the week was to be primarily one of *CELEBRATIONS*, and not just a week of fundraising. The second was that the *CHILDREN* were to be the centre of all the activities. It was recognised however that some funds were bound to flow into the coffers, and they certainly would not be refused!

Once the programme had been drawn up, a publicity campaign was launched, with notices to the press, radio, and television. All known ex-pupils were written to, asking them to please come along to the reunions and other events. Posters were made and displayed throughout the area so that hopefully nobody could ever say they didn't know about the anniversary.

The celebrations started on the Monday morning with a special service in the Church for all the pupils, staff, and anyone else who came along.

The School and Green Road had been bedecked with flags and bunting, and a festive spirit seemed to pervade all Meanwood. We took over the Meanwood Institute for the week, and Arthur Hopwood was in his element, having mounted a wonderful exhibition of old Meanwood photographs, maps, and memorabilia. There was a constant stream of visitors throughout the six days that it was open. There were souvenir and refreshment stalls, and they did a roaring trade.

After school hours on Monday we all made our way into Meanwood Park, which is adjacent to the school, for the first bit of fun and games. Two contests took place, the first being *'WELLIE WANGING.'* An area was roped off for security reasons, and a variety of wellington boots proved for the different age groups. The contest was of course to see who could throw a boot the farthest distance, and it soon became very obvious that it was not as easy as first thought. Technique seemed to beat brawn. There were prizes awarded to all the group winners, and as far as I know there were no direct hits by flying missiles. A jolly good laugh, but I don't think it will make the Olympics.

The second contest was *'THE LOUDEST VOICE IN MEANWOOD'*. For the bargain price of 50p. contestants were allowed three tries at shouting 'Happy Birthday Meanwood School' into a 'Sound Level Meter' an instrument for measuring the volume of the sound. We secured the services of Syd Bradley who was the Town Crier of Knaresborough to show us how it should be done, and he arrived all dressed in his colourful regalia to start the proceedings. He was a jolly character and kept things going at a lively pace. There were different age groups, and prizes for all the winners. Things became quite serious, with a number of contestants having multiple attempts trying to improve their techniques. The numbers of decibels were professionally monitored and recorded, and the secret seemed to be to finish with a high pitched crescendo. The advisability of doing this however came into question the following morning when sore throats were very much in evidence! The winners had to put up with a lot of ribbing, particularly the two young ladies who registered 104 decibels and came joint first. Would you like to carry the title of the loudest voice in the district? I will spare their blushes, and not mention the names of Bev or Noreen. The loudest of the lot was our youngest son Andrew with 109 decibels, and I can assure you that the fact that big brother David was taking the reading did not influence the situation at all! All the entrants received a certificate recording their decibel count.

Neither event made much profit, but provided a lot of hilarity, and got the week off to a flying start. Next morning the Yorkshire Post published an excellent photograph of the Town Crier and a boy contestant. One of the ideas behind having these events on the Monday was to try and get some good publicity for the rest of the week's festivities. It worked.

We decided to spread the reunions over three evenings to try and give everyone a chance to attend. It was a good job we did so, as there were excellent attendances. The three evenings were designated 'Under 30's', '30's to 50's,' and 'Over 50's' although we were not rigid. Countless cups of tea and coffee were consumed, and many a tale told as old pupils met up with former schoolpals, many of whom had not seen each other for many years. I think the lady from Canada who had carefully timed her holiday to be here for the anniversary had travelled the farthest distance. A lady of ninety turned up, all hale and hearty, and at the time we thought she must be the oldest ex-pupil, but were later proved wrong when Henry Shaw arrived on the scene. He was nearly a hundred, and later celebrated his centenary day in the school. It must be very good air in Meanwood!

The big event of the week was undoubtedly *VICTORIAN DAY* on the Wednesday. It turned out to be a lovely warm sunny day, and the children, staff, and some of the Committee all came dressed in Victorian style. Classes were conducted in the 'old fashioned' way, with rigid discipline and hands behind backs! I'm not sure what the children thought about that, but they all entered into the spirit of the occasion and had a good time. The highlight of the day was the visit of the Lord Mayor and Lady Mayoress, Councillor and Mrs Les Carter, who joined in the fun. They too came in Victorian dress. I had managed to persuade the Manager of the civic stables at Lotherton Hall to bring a horse and an old open carriage to bring the Mayoral party the last mile or so to the school. This duly turned up at the appointed meeting place, much to my relief. When the City's No.1 Limousine rolled up, the Lord Mayor, Lady Mayoress and myself climbed aboard the carriage to be driven in style through the streets of Meanwood, much to the surprise of some who were unaware of what was taking place, (albeit there couldn't have been many that could claim that). The police had stopped the traffic, and when we turned the corner and came in sight of the school the road seemed to erupt in a mass of cheering children, staff, parents and onlookers, all of whom seemed to be waving a Union Jack. I suppose that was the nearest I will ever be to feeling like royalty.

After disembarking, the Lord Mayor and Lady Mayoress did a 'walkabout' and spent a long time going around speaking to everyone. They were excellent. The bit the children loved most was when the Lord Mayor produced a cane, and proceeded to cane the rear end of the Director of Education, Stuart Johnson who fortunately entered into the spirit of fun. The local police had done their bit by sending two 'Bobbies' dressed in Victorian uniform to control the traffic and crowds

The V.I.P.'s were served with drinks in the headteacher's 'office', and it all went very well. The official party was then taken on a tour of the school, showing great interest in all the special activities going on in each of the classrooms. Then into the playground for Victorian songs, 'drill', dancing and games, supervised by Janet Burns from the Armley Mills Museum. A reporter from Radio Leeds turned up and made a live broadcast, and Yorkshire Television cameras took some footage. All good publicity. A lot of time and effort from the Staff had gone into training the children for the day's activities, Mums and Grans making all the costumes, and some of the Dads putting up street decorations. The result was a splendid day that all who were there will remember for a long time. Parents joined in the fun in the afternoon, and the school photographer set up a little studio and did a roaring trade taking family groups and photographs of the children in their Victorian costume.

A special anniversary brochure was produced, and 2,000 copies printed, and special anniversary mugs were made. Every child was given a brochure and a mug as they left school on Wednesday afternoon, and others were sold. The brochure contained a history of the school, plus a variety of photographs both old and new, and anecdotes of school life in the past. Some of the extracts from the Headmaster's log book made everyone realise what tremendous changes had taken place during the lifetime of the school, and more importantly, what further changes were urgently needed. Here are some examples;

Sept. 21st. 1903	*'...took standard 1 boys. Some very slow and listless and a few not even knowing their letters.'*
Dec.23rd. 1903	*'Distributed box of oranges and a barrel of apples kindly sent by Mr. Heeles (Manager) to the children'*
Mar. 21st. 1904	*'Physical exercises with the new dumb bells this afternoon.'*
Sept. 23rd. 1904	*'Spoke to the children about the growing evil of stonethrowing'*
Oct. 29th. 1904	*'Trafalgar Day. Had flag put out, and called the children together and spoke to them of 'Duty''*
April 27th. 1905	*' The attendance during the week is not at all good. Several children kept at home to assist in cleaning.'*
Sept. 28th. 1905	*'Very wet all day. Some of the children with poor boots were unable to come in the afternoon'*
Jan. 27th. 1906	*'Weather bitterly cold, and both main room and the two classrooms all below 40° temperature'*

How things have changed!

By the way . . . Do not print too many brochures. Better to be a few short and make them into sought-after collector's items!

On the Friday evening a *FANCY DRESS DISCO* was held in the Parochial Hall. This was organised by the Parents Association and a good time was had by all who attended, although I think by that time in the week a few of us were beginning to flag.

Saturday saw another very hectic day. In the afternoon a *ROUNDERS TOURNAMENT* was staged in the Park, whilst in our garden at Ivy Cottage we held a *TEDDY BEAR'S PICNIC*. You might well ask what was one of those? Well, for a modest entry charge you were admitted to the garden, and if you came complete with a Teddy of any shape, size, colour or condition you were given a large discount. The advertised opening time was 2p.m. but long before that, there was a massive queue winding down Green Road all clutching Teddy Bears of every description. Once the gates were opened they streamed in all afternoon, and we counted over 450 people, most of whom had a Teddy of some sort.

There were all the usual sort of garden party things going on such as Hoop-la, raffles, Tombola, sales of M.S.B.A. items, balloon race, cakestalls, guess the number of peas in the jar, guess the weight of the cake, refreshments, and a few special games. These were 'Pin the bow tie on Teddy,' and 'Find Teddy's Treasure.' In fact, anything that would bring in some cash and provide a bit of fun. The high spot of the afternoon was undoubtedly the judging of the various Teddy categories. Graham Walker one of the comedy team 'The Grumbleweeds' is an old Meanwood lad and kindly came along to do the judging. What a difficult and thankless task he had! There were prizes for the 'Biggest,' 'Cuddliest,' 'Smallest,' and 'Ugliest' and it raised more emotions than a Miss World competition. You would have thought that there were thousands of pounds at stake instead of our very modest prizes!

The result was a few went home very happy, and many went home disappointed, with quite a few tears shed.

I had dressed up for the afternoon in a clown's outfit for a bit of fun, and one of my jobs was to go around the stalls from time to time collecting cash and taking it away for safekeeping inside the house. My mother had noticed this, and went to find my wife to ask her if she knew that the clown kept disappearing into our house, and what an earth was he doing?

She had not recognised her own son all afternoon!

When it was all over we totted up the takings and found we had netted £461, which made a very busy afternoon well worth the effort.

Evening came, and we were off again, this time to the Parochial Hall for the 150th. *ANNIVERSARY SUPPER DANCE*. To be frank it was not one of the best events. I think we were all so tired after the week's activities that we hadn't enough energy left to let our hair down, and it never really got going. That was the only disappointment of the week though, so I reckon we didn't do too badly.' The Grand Draw', one of our major raffles was drawn during the evening by Graham Walker, so at least some people were satisfied.

Sunday morning brought us to the conclusion of the celebrations with a special *THANKSGIVING SERVICE* in Church, with an address by the Bishop of Knaresborough. I don't know who chose the hymns, and I certainly don't claim any of us were Saints, but the first one did seem appropriate . . . 'For all the Saints who from their labours rest.'

Overall, it was a splendid week, which gave us lots of welcome publicity and everyone had lots of fun, Incidentally we banked £1,136 for M.S.B.A. (plus profits from sales, etc., and a number of covenants were entered into).

Cathy reckons she put in 73 hours for M.S.B.A. during the week. I don't doubt it for a minute. It felt like much more!

And so to bed . . .

HENRY SHAW'S 100th. BIRTHDAY

Henry was 98 when we 'discovered' him, and was the oldest surviving ex-pupil of the school that we located. He had been a widower for many years, and still lived alone and looked after himself in a house at Stanningley. His niece Doreen Puckett 'kept an eye on him' and brought him to the School on a number of occasions. He took great delight in reciting tales about old Meanwood and his schooldays.

His 100th. birthday was on the 10th. May 1991 and we invited him to come to the School to celebrate the great event. The Lord Mayor, Bill Kilgallon, and the Lady Mayoress, came along to join in the fun and presented him with a Civic gift. The children gave him a monster birthday card, and a special birthday cake had been made, which Henry, as lively as ever, ceremoniously cut. The press turned up and published a delightful photograph of him talking to two of the children in the old playground.

We then retired to the headteacher's office for drinks and light refreshments. After the School Secretary had spilt a glass of lemonade down the Lord Mayor's suit, and then cleaned him up, Henry started again with his reminiscences. Doreen Wood took some cine film of the event and also made a tape recording. It went a follows;

> *'I started school at about three or four. When you first came you went up the steps to the infants class. The Headteacher lived in that cottage over there. It was a big day when you went into the big school.*
>
> *On the way home I used to go fishing and paddling in the beck. My mother used to play the devil with me for not going straight home to my dinner. Anyway she came to meet me one day when I was laiking in the beck, and she simply picked me up and chucked me in the beck. What needled me more than her chucking me in the water was that the leather workers were sat out having their dinner hour, and I was walking along wet through to the skin, my mother following me.*
>
> *When it was Queen Victoria's Jubilee we had a 'do' in Meanwood Beckett's Park. I won a race and got some little bantam wickets. My father won an alarm clock in a race.*
>
> *I left school when I was thirteen. It was a Wednesday. I went to school in the morning and didn't go back. In the afternoon I got a job, working in a greengrocer's shop at the top of Shaw Lane for three and a tanner a week. That was 1904, and £1 was a fair wage for a man. A big manager could earn thirty-five shillings.*

I've enjoyed my life, I think it's a long way to go, but I do miss friends from that time that I could talk to.'
Thank you Doreen for that delightful transcript of life long ago.

Henry died the following year, just before his 101st. birthday.

NOSTALGIA WEEKEND

We played the nostalgia theme for all it was worth. After the old school was closed, and the children had moved to Bentley Primary, but before the building work commenced, we organised a 'Nostalgia Weekend' in the empty School.

We invited as many ex-pupils as we could trace, and all those people on our database, and publicised the event widely. The School was open all day on the Saturday, and having the empty rooms, we were able to have a variety of displays and activities. In one room for example Doreen Wood with her cine films, and Martin Cockerill with his videos gave an almost continuous performance to an eager audience. In another room we concentrated on various games to keep the children occupied, and in the main hall we sold all manner of surplus items from the old School, plus the usual sales lines.

Displays of old class photographs, registers, and the old punishment book proved a big draw. Did the people who found their name in the punishment book feel proud or ashamed? (Listening to them afterwards I am sure it was the former!) Also displayed were the plans for the new school. Opportunities were provided for people to take out covenants, make donations, or enter into the dedicated giving scheme and quite a lot did so.

For 50p guests could sign the tablecloth that was later embroidered, or for the same princely sum ensure that their name went into the time capsule.

Later on we moved up to the Parochial Hall, where we staged a 'School Dinner and Evening of Nostalgic Entertainment.' A very light hearted affair. The meal was served by genuine school dinner ladies, but I am sure that the food was much better than I recollected from my schooldays. The concert highlight was the 'School Choir of Yesteryear' consisting of Frankie Dunderdale, Babs Blakeney, Dickie Holmes, Mary Dunderdale, and Richard Wiggen, all dressed in School uniform of course. It concluded with a rousing old-fashioned sing song.

To complete the weekend we held a special service in the Church, followed by refreshments in the Hall. Once again we had an appropriate hymn. 'One more step along the road we go.' It was a very big step, £2,290 to be precise!

FOUNDATION STONE CEREMONY

Friday 26th. June 1992 was a very special day. After all the frustrating planning delays and financial problems of the past years, the new School was finally beginning to take shape amidst the seeming chaos of the building site. We decided to conform to tradition and have a foundation stone-laying ceremony.

The stone was duly designed by the architect, and the order sent to the mason who carved the following inscription:

> THIS STONE WAS LAID BY
> THE LORD BISHOP
> OF RIPON
> ON 26th. JUNE 1992

Building work was in full swing, so obviously we could not give an open invitation to everyone to come along and see the ceremony. This presented a problem in deciding who should be invited. We finished up inviting the Patrons, The Director of Education, The Architect, the Builder, Staff, members of the M.S.B.A. Committee, and of course the Bishop. The children were represented by two from each class who came along and presented to the Bishop a scroll listing the names of all the children in their class. (These scrolls were eventually placed in the time capsule).

Arrangements had to be made for traffic control, 'No Parking' cones, safety fences, hard hats and lapel badges for all the visitors, a ceremonial trowel, publicity and a host of other bits and pieces. It was impractical to place the foundation stone in its final position, so the builders constructed a small temporary wall. The ceremony started with a number of speeches, and then the Bishop duly laid the Foundation Stone to the cheers of the assembled onlookers (which included quite a number peering over the wall). In due time the builders placed it in its final position, which is in the wall on the left hand side on the approach to the main School entrance doors. It is to be hoped that it will remain there for many a year to remind every one of that memorable day.

It was a beautiful summer's day, and after the ceremony we all retired to the garden at Ivy Cottage for light refreshments. In the evening we rounded off the day with an excellent barbecue in the Vicarage gardens.

OPEN DAYS

The long awaited day when the builders completed their task, and moved off site, came at Easter 1993. To mark the historic occasion, and to thank all our supporters, we held two open days. We invited all those on the database, (which had grown by this stage to over 1,000) and local residents, to come and see what had been achieved.

The first one was on Thursday, April 1st. when the School had just been handed over to us and everything was sparkling new. Between 500 and 600 guests turned up to see the completed building. We mounted displays of photographs showing how the work had progressed, and many others of the various events. We also displayed many of the posters that had been used for publicity, and looking at them made us realise what a tremendous effort had been put in by everybody connected with M.S.B.A. over the three and a half years.

Needless to say we had the usual refreshment and sales stalls, and gave people one last opportunity to make a dedicated gift, as fund raising was still continuing.

The second open day was quite a different occasion. It was on Saturday the 24th. April when the children had been back in occupation for three days. What a transformation! In some ways it seemed a shame to spoil the pristine building that we had seen previously, with piles of cardboard boxes, wall charts, and all the paraphernalia of a living School, (to say nothing of 180 boys and girls!) However that is what we had all been working for, happy children and staff in a first-class learning environment.

The Lord Mayor and Lord Grimthorpe came along together with about 750 visitors. A great and memorable day.

THE CELEBRATION

Following the virtual end of the successful fundraising campaign, and the School coming back into use, we tried to get a member of the Royal Family to come and officially open it. No luck, despite the efforts of Lord Grimthorpe and others. It was dragging on so long we decided to drop the idea, and rather than have an opening we would have a special CELEBRATION to mark the first anniversary of the re-opening.

This took place on Friday 22nd. and Saturday 23rd. of April 1994. The whole theme was one of celebration, and not fundraising for a change. Old habits die hard though, and some increase in the M.S.B.A. funds was noted!

Prior to the celebrations we had to tidy up a few bits and pieces. The Book of Dedications had to be completed to enable it to be put on display, and the original inscription on the bell tower had been eroded by the elements and needed sprucing up. It read;

> THIS SCHOOL
> AND THE MASTER'S HOUSE
> WERE BUILT BY
> CHRISTOPHER BECKETT ESQre
> OF MEANWOOD PARK
> IN THE YEAR OF OUR LORD
> MDCCCXL

We brought in a professional stone mason and had the lettering recut.

There were a number of other signs that we had to order and have fixed. These were 'William Lawies Jackson Hall' in recognition of the £10,000 donation from his estate, 'Dunderdale Court' in recognition of all the work Frank had done for the School over many years, 'The Thackray Room' acknowledging the donation from Charles Thackray, the medical equipment suppliers, and 'The Bewell Room'(no comment).

The celebrations commenced on the Friday morning with a special assembly in School to which parents and members of the Committee had been invited. We then went out into the courtyard where Lord Grimthorpe unveiled a new memorial stone in the wall outside the Headteacher's office. This read:

> This courtyard was named the
> Christopher Beckett Court
> By LORD GRIMTHORPE
> a descendant of the founder
> on 22nd. April 1994
> to commemorate the rebuilding
> of the School

In the afternoon it was the children's turn, and they had a whale of a time with their parties. In the evening we returned to the School and celebrated with a barbecue and bar in the Beckett Court.

For the Saturday we had sent out invitations to everyone that had contributed to the Appeal to come along during the morning and see what a wonderful new School they had helped to create. They turned up in their hundreds! The Book of Dedications took pride of place in the entrance lobby and there were queues looking at it to make sure their name was included. Thankfully we had not missed out anyone. The embroidered tablecloth was also on display and caused a lot of interest and admiration. Refreshments were served, and there were displays of photographs and posters showing many of the fund-raising events.

It was not just pieces of paper though. A School is all about children, and some of them came along to show us 'old fogies' what modern schooling is all about by demonstrating their skills on the computers, etc. There were samples of their projects all around the walls, and some of the girls and boys showed us how chess should be played by having games on the new outdoor set in the Dunderdale Court.

In the afternoon we threw the School open to all and sundry, and again had a very busy time. Everyone who came expressed their great satisfaction at what had been achieved. We had some special commemoration mugs made, and as you can imagine, they sold like hot cakes and will no doubt grace shelves in many homes for years to come as a reminder of those momentous years.

A happy and fitting celebration to mark the end of an era in Meanwood's history.

13

AN 'A TO Z' OF EVENTS

We had a wide variety of events throughout the three and a half years of the Appeal, some of which were little one-off events, and others were quite large affairs. On the following pages they are listed in alphabetical order for ease of reference. We didn't quite make one event for every letter of the alphabet, but were not far off!

ANNIE ALLSORTS PARTY

A sale of fancy goods and toys held in the School that was combined with a wine and cheese evening. In addition to the admission ticket money we were given a percentage based upon the sales, and of course made a bit extra on wine sales.

AEROBICS

See Sponsorship Chapter for details of this event.

AUCTION SALE

This turned out to be the best one-day money raising venture of the whole Appeal, with a final net profit of £3,188.

It was, however, a very labour-intensive exercise, particularly in the few days immediately preceding the sale, and of course on the day itself. Ian Jackson chaired the Sub-Committee and took on the onerous task of 'Event Director,' ably assisted by Dorothy Fenton, Jean Pearson, and Frank Dunderdale, all of whom had been involved in a similar event a few years previously. Their experience proved invaluable.

The first task was to settle on a date that did not clash with anything else in the area, and when the Parochial Hall was free. This had to be available, not only on the day of the sale, but for several days beforehand for storage facilities, and the day after to facilitate collections. This was not as easy as it seemed at first glance, but other users of the Hall were very accommodating.

4,000 leaflets were printed, and these were distributed to every house in the Meanwood area by the volunteer network delivery system. They were also sent, or dropped in at various antique and second hand shops over a wider area. These leaflets served a dual purpose. Firstly to appeal for goods to be donated, and secondly to publicise the event generally. Donors could state that all the sale proceeds could be retained by M.S.B.A., or they could choose to sell on a 50/50 basis. In fact nearly all donors chose the former method. Donors were requested to send in details as soon as possible, so that the catalogue could be prepared, but to hold on to the goods until a couple of days before the sale as we had nowhere in which to safely store them before then.

Posters were printed, and displayed around a wide area, and the press and local radio informed, so that all in all we obtained quite good coverage. This was borne out on the day when we had a capacity crowd in the Hall. Leaflets were distributed, and posters displayed, about a month before the big day.

The really hard work started a few evenings before the sale when a number of 'volunteers' were pressed into service to go around the district with 4 vans picking up the promised goods. These included a number of large items such as Victorian wardrobes and three piece suites, so there were a few choice expressions which I will not repeat here!

Worries were expressed about the vulnerability of the items when left in the Hall, particularly on the last night, when virtually everything would be there. Ian decided that some watchmen were required so he, together with Peter Smithson and Steve Clemmens, arranged to spend the night on the premises. Despite sleeping bags and cushions borrowed from the donated furniture, I understand that sleep was a bit elusive. This was officially put down to 1) Strange noises in the Hall. 2) Noisy snoring from one of the party. Personally I think that the pile of empty beer cans the next morning had something to do with it.

A catalogue had to be prepared as soon as all the items were to hand, and all the items given a lot number. This was a difficult last minute task, but thanks to the Vicarage photocopier working overtime, the job was completed ready for the first viewers. Altogether there were 358 items. That was the point when Ian realised that if it took one minute to auction each item, it would last six hours. He underestimated. The auctioning took seven and three-quarter hours!

There was a two hour viewing period before the sale started, and it was then that we realised our publicity had worked, as large numbers of people began rolling up.

There was a wide spectrum of goods, ranging from large furniture and bicycles, down to glassware, cutlery, china and jewellery. They were divided into sections, and an order of sale declared so that bidders had some idea when certain items would be coming up. Included in the items for auction were a number of things which we had been given to M.S.B.A. over a period, such as the signed photograph from the 'Darling Buds of May' television cast, a Wedgewood plate sent by the Lord Mayor, a book from Alan Bennett, some drawings and paintings from Mr. Parsons and two bottles of Vintage Port. The successful bidder for the wine brought me a sample a few days later, and it was delicious. One of the few perks of the job!

We were of course hoping for an odd Rembrandt, Picasso or Goya to turn up amidst the piles, and end all our worries. Alas, no such luck. One item though did pleasantly surprise us. It appeared to us to be an old wooden tray, but it turned out to be a much sought after 'Butler's Tray' and went to a dealer for about £150!

We had managed to obtain the services of a young professional auctioneer from one of the major auction houses free of charge, but unfortunately he turned out to be a bit dour, and not too fast, so the laughs were a bit thin on the ground. We also had a large force of helpers who were kept very busy throughout the afternoon. A doorman to take the admission money and distribute the catalogues, a cashier and assistant to handle all the incoming cash, stewards to handle each lot, and at least one person to keep an eye on security on each section, particularly on tables such as the jewellery and small goods.

Once things got cracking we soon all got the hang of the proceedings, but eight hours was a very long time! It was encouraging, though, to think that every time the gavel descended, money was flowing into the Appeal. It became quite exciting as the afternoon wore on as we realised it was going to be a highly successful affair.

The bidders ranged from the proverbial little old ladies to the professional dealers, and most seemed to go away happy with their new possessions. There were a few amusing moments. For example my wife had said during the viewing period that she rather fancied a particular set of cake stands. Like a true gentleman I started bidding when the lot came up, but unknown to me, my wife had also mentioned it to her mother and she too started bidding. Neither of us could see the other, and didn't realise what was going on until the price had gone up quite a bit. Never mind, I finished up with a happy wife, and it was all for a good cause! Another gentleman however was not so lucky. He had gone with strict instructions from his wife to bid for some particular item of chinaware. He patiently sat through most of the afternoon until his chance came, and he successfully placed his bid. Off he went home proudly carrying his prize, only to find out on presenting it to his wife that he had bid for the wrong piece of china. OOPS! One elderly man sat through most of the proceedings eager to see how much a painting of his would realise. I hope he was satisfied. I believe so.

At least the rather slow proceedings meant that the refreshment stall did a roaring trade that helped the total along. This also helped to defray the lost profit on a nice little bedside cabinet that one of the stewards sat upon during the afternoon. It collapsed and had to be withdrawn from the sale!

When the whole thing was over, and the cashiers had totted it all up, the cash was taken down to the nightsafe and left there for the weekend. So far so good, but on Monday morning when we went in to sort it all out, the Manager could not find the key to open the nightsafe wallet and we had to wait a week before it could be finalised.

After the auction was completed there was a lot of clearing up to be done ready for the Sunday School the next morning, and somehow we had to store some of the items for collection, but we managed it without too much inconvenience. The few items that were not sold were retained by us and turned into cash later in various ways. One little lad had seen a music centre that he had set his heart on, but unfortunately for him it did not reach its reserve and was withdrawn. The next day he rang me and made a very low offer that I politely refused, but over the next few days he rang several more times, each time with a slightly better offer, until I eventually gave up and let him have his bargain. It was certainly a case of persistence winning the day as far as he was concerned.

TIPS

Make sure you engage a first class experienced auctioneer.
Do not accept 'junk.'
Steer clear of electrical goods if possible.
Make sure all bidders pay for their goods there and then.
Insist all goods are cleared immediately after the sale ends, or at the latest within 24 hours.

Happy bidding!

BARN DANCES

A number of these were held, and they proved popular with all ages. The first one was organised by Glynis Shaw and featured a live band, appropriately named 'The Village Band,' who came from Derbyshire. Over 100 revellers enjoyed the evening and we were better off to the tune of £331. The bar sold 'Real Ale' and this seemed to be as big an attraction as the dancing! Others were held later such as 'The Harvest Barn Dance' and we always included a supper and a bar.

It is essential to have experienced callers who know all the dances and can instruct people with two left feet such as myself. A good way to let off steam.

BEETLE DRIVE

We organised a 'Santa's Beetle Drive' at the Hall one Saturday afternoon just before Christmas. Although it was a very snowy day with driving almost impossible, twenty hardy enthusiasts turned up and had a thoroughly enjoyable time. A lot of the younger ones didn't know what it was all about, but soon got into the swing of things. One lady confessed later that she hadn't come because she thought it was something to do with a 'Beetle' car, and hers was a Ford. (If you believe that, you will believe anything!)

BARBECUES

These proved very popular, and we held quite a number. Venues were the Vicarage garden, Ivy Cottage garden, The Myrtle Beer Garden, and right at the end, one in the new School courtyard.

The one at Ivy Cottage was arranged by the Meanwood Village Association, and we did all our own catering and cooking which made a big difference to the final profit. The fact that a friend of mine owned a beefburger factory also helped! Another case of knowing the right people.

TIPS

The requirements for a large barbecue are as follows;
A large barbecue. (In our case I built one.)
Cooking tools.
Charcoal, special lighting fuel, matches or lighter. (Take care.)
One or two experienced barbecue chefs. (The scouts are good at this.)

Barn Dance Poster

> *Beefburgers (top quality), sausages, bread rolls, salads, sauces, salt and pepper,*
> *Alternative food for the increasing number of vegetarians.*
> *Bar supplies i.e. drinks, glasses, corkscrew, bottle opener, ice and bucket, price list, and last but not least a good barmaid or barman.*
> *Large kettles, teapots, coffee pots, tea, coffee, sugar, cups, and spoons.*
> *Plates and cutlery. (I think plastic permissible in this case).*
> *Serviettes.*
> *Containers for hot food. (School dinner type).*
> *Outside lighting. (Take care on safety aspect).*
> *Rubbish receptacles.*
> *Toilet facilities.*
> *Seats and tables.*
> *Weather protection, at least over the barbecue.*
> *Arrange a raffle or some other little moneyspinner.*
> *Finally, get the fire going well before the starting time.*

BELL RINGING

Always on the lookout for the unusual, we had a bell ringing evening in the Church. This consisted of a concert by the Seacroft Handbell Ringers, and a talk by Dr. Maurice Calvert, the Captain of the Bells of Meanwood Parish Church. Both proved very interesting. Afterwards, the ones who considered themselves fit and healthy were given a chance to prove it by climbing the bell tower. Most thought it well worth the effort, but the remainder were too puffed to express an opinion!

Another little idea that brought in a few pounds occurred when the School was complete, and we had an open day. Visitors with 50p. to spare could ring the School bell, which was housed in the refurbished bell tower. It proved to be a popular attraction, but I'm not too sure what the neighbours thought. Incidentally the bell is now rung at the beginning and end of every school day by one of the children.

BURNS NIGHT CELEBRATIONS

Iain and Anne Burgess organised an excellent evening in the Parochial Hall, which made a profit in excess of a thousand pounds. The haggis had been caught, killed and cooked in time-honoured fashion before being piped into the room by a piper in full highland dress. He was followed by the all important stewards carrying the whisky, salt and bread. The piper performed the ceremony of cutting the haggis and reciting the traditional ode.

Before all this pomp and ceremony there had been a little hiccup, however. The 'tatties and neeps' which are served with the haggis were being prepared during the afternoon. After cooking the Tatties, they were mashed, by being put through the mincer, but they seemed to be going through a bit too slowly, so the cooks, (who shall be nameless for fear of a libel action!) decided to give them a help by pressing them down with the handle of a wooden spoon. Alas the machine grabbed the spoon and shredded a good inch of it into the Tatties. A debate followed as to whether or not to confess and start again, or to hell with it and serve it up as it was. Fortunately for the guests they started again!

After everyone had taken their fill of the feast, and washed it down with a few drams of the hard stuff, we were treated to a demonstration of Scottish dancing, and then all had to join in. (With varying degrees of success). Several of the male guests had come along in the kilt, and some of the ladies in traditional dresses and sashes, which helped to make a very colourful evening. A very enjoyable and profitable event.

BINGO

Not a lot you can say about normal bingo, except that it is a very simple way to make money, but have you ever played or heard about stand-up bingo? Sometimes called Dutch bingo.

It is an unbelievably easy way to make a lot of money in a few minutes. It does not make an event in itself, but can be slotted in during an interval at a dance or quiz night. It works like this. Sell bingo cards around the room in the normal way, and then ask all the participants to stand up. Spin the balls, and then the caller starts shouting out the numbers. As soon as a number is called, anyone with that number on their card sits down. The last one standing scoops the prize.

A hundred pounds in the kitty in less than ten minutes!

CAKE STALLS

We had the good fortune to have amongst our faithful supporters a number of ladies who not only loved baking, but also enjoyed having a stall to sell their produce. Cathy Holding, Ann Fairy, Elaine McGee and the inseparable twins Ida Snow and 'Aunty Ada' did a marvellous job for M.S.B.A. and must have baked thousands of cakes, buns, scones and the like. Their stall was always the first to sell out. The funds swelled, but so unfortunately did our waistlines!

CAR BOOT SALE

Luckily for us Sunday trading had not started at the time, so we were able to persuade the local supermarket to give us the unrestricted use of their carpark one Sunday morning. Janet Thornton headed up the team for this event, and dealt with the licence application, bookings, refreshments, etc. We advertised over a wide area some weeks before the event, and this resulted in quite a number of places being prebooked.

We arranged for a large number of marshals to be on duty, and it was a good job we did. Long before the advertised opening time for stallholders, people were queuing up at the entrance demanding instant admission, and the bargain hunters too were rolling up in their hundreds, although the official opening of the sale was some couple of hours hence! The marshals did their best to control the situation, but in the end they admitted defeat and the mob surged in. It was all stations go! It was amazing to watch as the buyers surrounded each car as it rolled up, and were trying to barter for the goods before they were even unloaded. The roads for a large area around the supermarket were chock-a-block with cars and vans, but somehow it all sorted itself out without any mishaps.

Profits came from selling refreshments, pitch 'rentals', sales of concessions for stalls selling food and drinks and what we sold off our own stalls (£144 of 'junk'). It was amazing what people bought. At the end everyone seemed to be going away with large bags crammed with everything under the sun, and big smiles on their faces. The stallholders also appeared happy, and our treasurer was beaming when he banked the £766 profit, so it seems everyone had a good day. Except Cathy that is, who dislikes that sort of event, and described it as "a jumble sale with woodworm!"

The weather man smiled on us too, at least during the sale, but as soon as it had ended the heavens opened, and the helpers who were clearing up got a soaking. At that time it didn't really seem to matter, and nobody complained. An hour later you could not tell we had been there, which was very important for our relationship with the supermarket.

As well as a lot of happy buyers and sellers it turned out to be quite a jolly social occasion.

CAROL SINGING

You can't really lose on this one. All you need is a number of volunteers, a little organisation, and a lot of cheek in rattling your tin under everyone's nose.

Doreen Wood and Carolina Brook arranged a few sessions around houses in Meanwood, and even if we didn't make a fortune we like to think we brought a touch of Christmas to some people.

We also obtained permission to sing carols in the main concourse at Leeds City Station for a couple of hours. That was a real bucket rattling session, and we did quite well, particularly when there was a hold up of some sort and a big queue developed right in front of us. All we had to do was walk along the line of the 'captive audience'. Unfortunately not many singers turned up, which made it rather hard work for the ones that did.

Carol concerts were organised in the Church on the last Saturday afternoon before Christmas each year, and these proved very popular. I am not sure whether the congregation came to sing carols, for the sherry and mince pies that were served at the end, or just wanted an excuse to get out of going shopping. The schoolchildren were involved, which is always a good idea, because you have a guaranteed congregation of mums, dads, and grandparents. M.S.B.A. benefited nicely from the retiring collections.

CHEESE AND WINE EVENINGS

We held a variety of such evenings at different venues, and organised by different groups, such as the Mothers Union, the Meanwood Village Association and Stainbeck United Reformed Church. Although not big moneyspinners, contributions such as these were invaluable, not only for the cash they generated, but for the fact that they involved different sections of the Community. They can be combined with other events.

Quite easy to organise, but as usual the success depends on the enthusiastic selling of tickets beforehand, and good publicity.

CINE SHOWS

Doreen Wood our local cine enthusiast made a number of films recording our various activities, and these were always well received when shown later. They also made a permanent record, for the future generations to see how we did our fundraising in the nineties.

Doreen put on a number of shows including 'Our Village 1977-1990' and 'Our Village School' in addition to showing her famous squirrel sequences.

CRICKET MATCH

Another example of how to have a nice Sunday afternoon's entertainment, and make a pound or two in the process. Ian Jarvis arranged a match between a Parents' X1 and a Meanwood Cricket Club X1 on Meanwood's pitch at the Myrtle Tavern. Players paid for the privilege of entertaining the crowd, and this was topped up by the sale of refreshments and a raffle. We also had a bouncy castle for the children that was sponsored by a local company and proved as popular as ever. Lots of fun, and I can't remember who won, but it didn't really matter, because M.S.B.A. certainly won to the tune of £186.

CREAM TEAS

Another affair that didn't help the waistline. Some of the ladies arranged afternoon cream teas at the Parochial Hall that brought in another £106.

COFFEE MORNINGS / AFTERNOONS / EVENINGS

Numerous individuals and organisations did their bit for the Appeal by arranging coffee mornings, afternoons, or evenings at all sorts of venues. Simple to arrange, but again you have to entice the customers in. Not content with these simple affairs someone came up with an idea that they said was 'guaranteed' to bring in millions and end all our worries. It was a 'Snowball Coffee' scheme.

All we had to do was to persuade one person to hold a coffee morning at their house, and invite two guests, who obviously paid for their coffee. The two guests then had to go away and each arrange a coffee morning at their house and invite three guests. Those six went away and invited four guests each, and so on, and so on.

In THEORY inside a few weeks we should have been rolling in money. The originator however had somehow forgotten to build into the calculations the fact that very soon everyone in Meanwood (and that is about 10,000) would have been to a coffee morning, afternoon, or evening, and would be suffering from caffeine poisoning! Anyway it got a few laughs and brought in a bob or two.

CONCERTS

A number of concerts were held in the Church and the Chapel that proved quite popular. Again ticket selling and publicity were vital to the success. We discovered that all the singers, bands, and choirs had a regular group of enthusiastic followers, and these made a significant contribution to the ticket sales. It was therefore important to send a quantity of tickets to them to sell a week or two before the event. In addition to the admission monies we always had our sales stall set up, a refreshment stall, donation jars around, and publicity material on display about the Appeal in general and forthcoming events.

We also found out that many of the bands, orchestras, and choirs were always on the lookout for opportunities to perform for good causes, and in good venues, on an expenses-only basis. All we had to do was ask. It was then just a matter of settling dates and organising the event.

Concerts were performed by the following;

Leeds Intermediate Concert Band	(£300 profit)
The Bradford Choristers	(£169)
The Yorkshire Post Brass Band	(£465)
The West Riding Singers	(£110)
The Lawnswood Singers	(£150)

There were also the two performances of the Messiah by the St. Peter's Singers. (See the Sponsorship chapter).

CYCLING

See sponsorship chapter for details of this event.

DANCES

Not one of the Writer's favourite occupations, but many people enjoyed the variety of dances and discos that were held throughout the Appeal. We tried to suit all age groups, generally with success.

We had one big disappointment however, which turned out to be the biggest flop of the campaign. We were offered the free use of the Banqueting Suite in the Leeds Civic Hall to hold an 'Easter Ball', and started the publicity wagon rolling with tickets being priced at £15 per head, including supper. So as not to preclude anyone without a dress suit or ball gown we decided to make it a 'Lounge suit' affair. The ticket sales were very poor, so we started to ask people why they were not supporting the event. Some of the reasons given surprised us. "What do you mean by a lounge suit?" and "I haven't got a lounge suit, and it would mean hiring one" We continued to try and sell the tickets, but in the end we had to admit defeat and cancel it 10 days or so beforehand, and give refunds. We went wrong somewhere... Oh well, back to the £2.50 disco!

The most popular was the 'Fifties Night'. This referred to the era of the music, not the age of the dancers, by the way. We had a live band of two very talented dads, and three of their friends, plus wives acting as vocal backing. Very popular with many of the parents, who came along in their fifties rigouts and indulged in an evening of nostalgia. It made £615.

One event with a difference, was the 'Slave Auction and Disco' that was held in the Meanwood Working Men's Club. Prior to the event we asked people to offer their skills and services in aid of the Appeal, which on the night were auctioned. The offers came rolling in, but unfortunately there was a poor attendance on the night, so that not all the offers were taken up. However some were sold in the following few days.

The offers included;

Half a day's heavy gardening.
Three nights' baby sitting.
Two hours' sewing.
Transporting to and from a night out.
Two hours' handyman work around the house.
Car valeting.
Cleaning windows.
Light removals in 15 mile area.
Rotavating a garden.
Making up a bouquet of flowers.

Decorating a room.
Washing and ironing.
Cleaning a cooker.
Baking a novelty cake.
Shopping for pensioner.
Dog walking.
Fortune telling.
Two hours' weeding.
One hour riding lesson.
Making up a dress.

I finished up at a house in Headingley painting 7 doors for a tenner!

DOGWALK

See Sponsorship chapter for details of this event.

FASHION SHOWS

Very popular with the ladies, as you would imagine. A number were held including 'Second Thoughts' and 'Elite Fashions'. These were usually combined with a wine and cheese evening. The profits came from ticket money, sale of extra wine and a percentage based on the sales made.

The Meanwood Ladies Group put on a Fashion Show of their own that brought in over £300.

FLOWER FESTIVAL

This was one of the big moneyspinners, putting over £1,600 into the M.S.B.A. coffers. It was held in the Meanwood Parish Church, and fully organised by them, over a long bank holiday weekend.

An enormous effort was made by some of the Church members in the weeks prior to the Festival, in designing and creating the frameworks, etc. for all the wonderful displays. Then in the couple of days before it opened it was very hectic indeed, buying and arranging all the flowers. The final result was beautiful.

The Festival was publicised widely, and resulted in a number of visiting parties from churches some distance away, as well as hundreds of local people. It commenced on the Friday evening with a preview and a wine and cheese evening. On the Saturday the Church was open all day, followed by a musical evening, and further viewing took place on Sunday afternoon and Bank Holiday Monday.

Profits arose from donations, sale of the programmes, refreshments, ticket sales for the Friday and Saturday evening events, and our old faithful . . . the sales stall.

A very memorable and profitable Festival weekend.

FORTUNE TELLING

A bit of fun at one of the events, when we set up a 'Gypsy' tent and charged for people to have their fortunes told. We were staggered at the popularity of it, and at one stage we had to tell the dear old 'Gypsy' to speed it up a bit as the queues were too long. We never found out how accurate the forecasts turned out!

FAIRS

The Parochial Church Council held a fair each autumn, and they generously decided to donate their profits to the Appeal during the fund raising years.

A lot of hard work went into each fair in the weeks preceding the event, and of course a tremendous imput on the day itself. There were all the usual games, garden produce stalls, bookstalls, tombola, refreshments, raffles, competitions, displays by the children, and anything at all that would induce visitors to part with their cash! Each year seemed to bring out another ingenious game for doing so.

The net result was a lot of happy visitors, a lot of exhausted staff and helpers and a very happy treasurer who had in excess of £1,000 to bank.

FOOTBALL

A number of tournaments were held each season, each of which helped the funds along, as well as providing lots of keen competition amongst the boys and girls. (Yes, some of the girls are just as keen as the boys). Some matches were also played with mixed parent and child teams.

FUN RUN

See Sponsorship chapter for details of this event.

GANG SHOW

The Guides from the Church made their contribution by putting on a Gang Show in the Parochial Hall. They provided a good evening of entertainment and handed over to M.S.B.A. the profits amounting to £105.

GREEK NIGHT

An excellent event held in the Parochial Hall, and attended by 130 people (the maximum allowed in the Hall). The evening was arranged by the Moutsakis family, Chris Croft, and others with Greek connections and they laid on Greek food, Greek wines, and a team of Greek dancers. The dancers demonstrated a variety of traditional Greek dances, and then of course we all had to join in. This event raised over £700, and proved so popular that another evening was put on the following year with a similar profitable result. Just before one of the demonstrations, Janice, who was wearing Greek national dress with an above-the-knee skirt, put her knee through her tights. No panic, just a quick change in the loo with Cathy who was fortunately wearing a long dress. They did get a few queer looks though as they emerged from the loo together!

HENRY SHAW'S 100th. BIRTHDAY

See Special Events chapter for details.

THE HUNDRED CLUB

Janet Thornton masterminded and ran this one by persuading just over a hundred people to pay 25p. per week into the club. There was a weekly draw with a cash prize of £5, a monthly draw for £15 and one every quarter for a mind boggling £25! Not quite up to National Lottery levels, but a bit of harmless fun. No licence is required, but the rules say that at least half the income has to be given back in prize money. The only problem was that I never made it onto the winner's list. In the first year alone it brought in a profit of £990. It was good money, but a lot of chasing around for Janet and her 'agents', but she carried on and repeated it the next year.

JUMBLE SALES

Someone once said that everyone should go to at least one jumble sale in their life to complete their education. Well, I had never been involved in one until M.S.B.A. came along, but I soon realised what had been meant by that remark.

What an eye opener that first one was! I wasn't sure whether to put this item under 'Sales' or 'Entertainments,' but decided that the latter was the most appropriate. It is of course an early example of what we nowadays call recycling, so I suppose there is a certain amount of satisfaction in that aspect of them. It is also a superb place to observe human nature, with one person's rubbish becoming another's prize.

On one occasion a rather scruffy chap came in wearing a ground-length old greatcoat, and proceeded to rummage amongst the piles when a telephone rang. He opened his coat, took out his mobile phone (a bit of a novelty in those days) and carried on what was obviously a business conversation in very cultured tones. He then popped it back, buttoned up his coat and continued looking for bargains!

On another occasion a lady came in, took off her coat, sat on the front of the stage in full view of everyone and calmly breast fed her child.

There was a bit of a flap one day when a lady protested loud and long that there was a thief around and her purse had been stolen. She demanded to know what we were going to do about it? An awkward situation, but we tactfully asked her to check her bag before we called the police. Lo and behold there it was at the bottom of her shopping bag. Exit one embarrassed lady, and peace returned.

Perhaps a few tips might not come amiss here;

Book the Hall in good time.

Advertise widely, including notifying the second-hand and antique shops.

Arrange for somewhere to store the goods in the couple of weeks prior to the event. Someone usually has a spare garage or room. (If not you will just have to park your Rolls Royce on the drive outside for a spell).

Collect as much as you can. Anything goes.

Have plenty of helpers on the day to sort the things out and set up the stalls.

On no account open the doors before the advertised time, and don't look out of the window at the assembling crowds or you will run a mile. They look like an attacking regiment.

Have a beefy man on the door to take the admission money, and make sure the entrance is only wide enough for one, or at the most two people to come in at a time. Even a modest entrance charge of 10p or 20p will be evaded if possible by the surging mass.

All the stalls must be properly manned before the doors open. The first target is usually the odds and ends stall where they will all be looking for that treasure that they saw last week on the 'Antiques Road Show'. Alas, they will more than likely be disappointed, but keep looking yourself.... these things do happen sometimes.

Have a discreet roving 'Security man' keeping an eye on the ones with large bin bags. It is surprising how quickly a dozen items can be stuffed into one, and 10p offered to the stallholder "for these two in the bag love." He should also keep collecting the currency notes from the stallholders from time to time.

Keep the prices low if you want to turn over the goods. The punters only want to pay 10p for anything anyway.

> *Do not try and sell any new goods at the same time. It is impossible to obtain a fair price. One of the few events when we didn't have the usual sales stall.*
>
> *If any decent items are sent in, pull them out before the sale, and sell them on another occasion when a fair price can be obtained.*
>
> *Do not forget the refreshment stall to pull in a few extra pounds. (As well as providing a welcome cuppa for the helpers).*
>
> *Make sure all the helpers put their belongings in a separate locked room. I know it's a standing joke about the helper's coat being sold, but it can happen. In fact, I am told it did, on more than one occasion!*
>
> *When the doors close I am convinced that there are always bigger piles of jumble than when it started. I am sure it breeds in that couple of hours. Disposal is the next problem. If you are having another one in the not too distant future, store the stuff if possible, otherwise arrange for a dealer to be there at the close and take the lot. You will not get much for it, but it will save you having to dispose of it all yourself.*

We held quite a few for the Appeal, and the average net profit was in excess of £200. Well worth the effort, and another provider of a bit of fun. Happy Jumbling!

LAUNCH

See Special Events chapter for details.

MESSIAH

See Sponsorship chapter for details of this event.

NOSTALGIA WEEKEND

See Special Events chapter for details.

NETBALL

Various sponsored tournaments were held which encouraged the girls, and brought some more cash in.

OPEN GARDENS

The gardens at Ivy Cottage are at their best in the springtime, with a continuous carpet of colour for weeks on end. It starts with the snowdrops and crocus, followed by daffodils and tulips and finishing with a mass of bluebells.

Each spring during the Appeal we opened the gardens up to visitors most weekends, and many people took advantage of a walk around instead of peering over the fence as they had done in previous years. We did not charge for admission, or for the refreshments served in the conservatory, but left donation jars and leaflets around. This proved quite profitable, and better than charging a fixed sum. There was only one exception to the generosity of people, and that was when a couple of passing lads saw the sign outside and took up our offer of free refreshments with a vengeance. They had a 'beano' until we had to call time! On our best day we made £35.

OPEN DAYS

See Special Events chapter for details.

PATE AND PLONK LUNCH

Another event at Ivy Cottage. It took place one Sunday in December 1991, and we made a net profit of £170. It was a simple affair, all we had to do was provide a selection of Pates, fresh crusty bread, salads, a sweet, a variety of wines, soft drinks, tea and coffee, together with the appropriate crockery and cutlery.

The main problem was how to fit everybody in, and provide them with seats. It was surprising how many we did squeeze in, and by borrowing various chairs, and the benches from school everybody was fed and watered in passable style.

QUIZ NIGHTS

Another very popular type of evening's entertainment. Several were held at the Parochial Hall and the Conservative Club, with each one contributing several hundred pounds to the Appeal.

Quiz Night Poster

The usual publicity and early ticket sales were the first priority, but then the main problem was in pitching the level of questions. They had to be at a level whereby everyone had a chance of answering them correctly, but not too easy so that everyone got them all right. Tricky.

The room was set out with tables for six or eight people. Some people would form teams of friends beforehand, and take the whole thing very competitively, whereas others would just form ad hoc teams on the night and have a good laugh. The evening would start off with a written quiz on each table, which kept people occupied until everyone was in place. This was handed in and marked during the second interval and a prize awarded to the winning table. The main quiz then started which usually consisted of three or four rounds, with a supper break in the middle. The bar of course ran continuously!

A good P.A. system was essential, as there was usually a fair amount of chattering going on, particularly as the evening progressed. The quizmaster would read out each of the ten questions in a round, giving time on each one for the members in a team to confer before writing down their answers. One member from each team would then take the answer to the quizmaster for marking. After each round the team marks would be chalked up on a large board so that everyone could see how their team was progressing. There were prizes for the winning team in each round, and then a major prize for the overall winners.

In the interval we would have either a couple of rounds of stand-up bingo, or another very easy moneyraising game. This consisted of clearing an area of dance floor, i.e. a slippy surface, and standing a bottle of whisky at one end. Competitors would then stand behind the starting line and slide coins along the floor towards the bottle. There would be a strict time limit of say ten minutes, and at the end of that time the nearest one to the bottle won it. A good keen eyed 'referee' is essential at the bottle end. We used old ten pence coins in those days and it was necessary to have a good supply of change for the punters. It is surprising how much money can slide down in ten minutes.

RAFFLES

See separate chapter on Raffles.

ROUNDERS

Helen Cockerill, Bev Simpson and Yvonne Jarvis organised a number of adults' rounders matches in Meanwood involving teachers, parents, and supporters. The total profits amounted to over £250, and it was typical of the small successful events that made such an important contribution to the Appeal.

Players had to pay for the privilege of taking part and amusing the spectators with their skills, (or should I say antics?) I also understand there was a bit of betting went on under the trees, but as the bookies' profits went into the M.S.B.A. pot I'll say no more! They were very enjoyable afternoons despite some stiff muscles next day. At least in my case.

Not specifically connected with these matches, but a little tale that did the rounds. A lady called in the police to investigate "Mysterious circles that had appeared in the grass in Meanwood Park" This was at the height of a national 'Corn circles mystery' attributable to U.F.O.'s. They turned out to be the areas which the Parks Dept. had just cut for the Schools sports!

RACE NIGHTS

These evenings were in the big league and ever popular. Bev and Gordon Simpson were the leading lights. One was held in the Parochial Hall , and two in the Meanwood Working Men's Club, and the profits amounted to £700, £892, and £1,006 respectively. A grand contribution.

During the evening there are eight genuine horse races shown on the screen, and betting takes place in the same way as on a racecourse and proves very exciting. The films, projector, screen, operator and M.C. can all be hired for the evening, but Gordon and Bev had a good friend who generously provided it all for free.

When the films arrive there are about a dozen of them in unmarked sealed canisters, and just before the race, and when the betting has closed, a member of the audience is invited to choose one at random. This ensures complete fairness, with not even the projectionist knowing what is to be shown. The odds are worked out before the race starts, on the basis of how much has been bet on each horse, and the payout calculated, which is approximately 50% of the bets taken. All the races have obviously been selected for their excitement value, and the horse which is leading early on in the race rarely wins, and there are a lot of neck and neck finishes.

The moneyraising however starts long before the night, with invitations being issued to local businesses and individuals to sponsor and name one of the races for £10 each. Invitations are also given to buy and name one of the eight horses in each of the races at £2 a time. So before the evening starts there is a fair amount in the kitty, with the added advantage that some of the money has come in from people who may not be attending the function. A printed race card is distributed which shows the names of all the horse and race sponsors.

As the evening nears its end, and assuming the bar has been well used, the time has come to auction the horses in the last race. Their names and pedigrees have already been chosen, and entered on the race card, and these alone can provide a lot of amusement. For example 'Shocking Experience, by Electrician, out of Luck', and 'Safety Pin, by Knickers, out of Elastic.' Sometimes the censor has to be brought in! Good prizes are essential for this final race, and it usually turns out very exciting and noisy. The lucky person who bought the winning horse in the auction gets 50% of the total sales of those 8 horses.

Quite a lot of money changes hands on each race, and the winning sponsor of each race receives say a bottle of champagne.

A FEW TIPS

Book a large room in plenty of time, and have ample tables and chairs.

Book the films and equipment. (They will usually send betting slips also.)

Organise a good bar and staff.

Make sure you have a good M.C. and sound equipment, as the punters can get a bit rowdy!

Probably the most important of all is to have a first class team of bookies' clerks who are numerate, quick, and SOBER. as in the short period between races they have a lot to do, taking bets on the next race and paying out on the previous one. You need at least four tables, with a pair of clerks on each.

Ensure a cash float is available with the appropriate change.

Finally, take care with the cash on the way to the nightsafe.

Happy punting.

RUNNING

See Sponsorship chapter for details.

SAFARI SUPPER

A nice June evening saw about 70 supporters walking around the area looking very satisfied, and so they should. They were participating in a Safari Supper. Tickets were sold in advance as usual, and particularly in this case, so that the catering numbers were known in advance. The costs had all been sponsored by certain individuals, so the profits were assured.

The starter course was served in the schoolroom at Meanwood Methodist Church, and then guests walked about a quarter of a mile up to the Parochial Hall, hopefully working up an appetite on the way. Here they were given the main course before proceeding another half mile or so downhill (thankfully!) to Ivy Cottage on Green Road, where a sweet and coffee finished off a very pleasant evening.

The requirements were simply three good venues, food, drink, volunteers to prepare, serve and clear up, and hey presto, another lot of satisfied customers and £289 in the pot.

SANTA'S GROTTO

Another little event that brought the crowds rolling in one Christmas was Santa's Grotto.

After school hours, on a couple of afternoons during the last week of term, Santa, complete with his faithful fairy attendants, took up residence in the conservatory at Ivy Cottage, much to the delight of the 141 excited children who came to see him. It started off, as a lot of events did, with a chance remark and quickly grew into a full-scale affair.

We were overwhelmed by the demand for tickets, and long before the advertised opening time there were jostling queues outside the gate. In addition to the children, there were untold numbers of mums, dads, and grandparents, so the house was bursting at the seams. The true identity of Santa is, of course, a well-kept secret. Let us just say he did a grand job as usual. Once, when I walked into the room, a little girl expressed great surprise, and said she was so sure it was me in the Grotto under the cloak and white beard. I explained that this year we had managed to get the real Santa to call in at Meanwood. Exit small girl with puzzled expression!

The Grotto had been made out of an old tent trimmed up with fairy lights, balloons, etc. and looked very effective. All the children received a small gift from Santa. The parents, if they could fight their way through the crowd, managed a cup of tea or coffee. As always, we tried to make a bit extra, in this case by having a cake stall in the dining room, and also selling sprigs of berried holly out of the garden. We finished up with £151 for M.S.B.A.

SILENCE

See Sponsorship chapter for details.

SLIDE SHOWS

We held a number of slide shows and travel talks. The first one was in the School, and was a very interesting and amusing talk by Chris Knamiller about a trip to Bhutan. It netted £45.

David Brook, one of the parents, and a well known caver, gave the second one. This time it was in the Methodist Church, and entitled 'The Caves of Mulu'. I unfortunately had to miss this one, but I understand it was excellent, concerning his exploration of a massive cave system in Borneo. It brought in £109.

I put on two shows in the Parochial Hall. The first one being an account of an expedition to Africa in which I had recently taken part. I called it 'African Adventure' and it covered my trials and tribulations on the ascent of the highest mountain in Africa, Mount Kilimanjaro, followed by experiences on a camping safari around Tanzania. It seemed to be well received, and we made £183. My second proved so popular that I had to organise a second showing the following week at the Methodist Church to supply the demand for tickets. These two evenings made £477 between them. This show was entitled 'Fire and Ice' and covered my camping safari around the wild and rugged splendours of Iceland. Never one to miss a chance of some extra profit, I contacted the travel company that I had gone with, and suggested that for a small donation I would be willing to give their company a 'plug' and distribute their literature. They agreed, and a pile of brochures were soon on my doorstep, together with a cheque for £50.

A good projection and sound system are very important, particularly if it is a large room, and blackouts, or at least curtains are essential. Plenty of space is also useful to set out the sales tables, and refreshments.

In addition to these shows in Meanwood I went around various societies and clubs in West Yorkshire showing one of these, or another show entitled 'Himalayan Trek.' Each one brought in a 'fee' to M.S.B.A. of £25.

Slide Show Poster

SLIMMING
SNOOKERTHON
SWIMMING
See Sponsorship chapter for details of these events.

TALK

Alan Pedley, a member of the Committee, and Honorary Alderman of the City of Leeds, arranged an evening's entertainment at the Parochial Hall during which everyone heard his amusing and interesting stories about his wartime experiences as a Sunderland flying boat pilot.

Afterwards we had a Pie and Peas Supper and the raffling of a special European edition of Monopoly which Alan had coaxed out of his friend at Waddingtons. A very profitable evening that increased the bank balance by £510.

TOMBOLA

One of the first money raising ventures of the Appeal was when Ian and Margaret Jackson had a Tombola stall at Yorkshire Water's Open Day at West Park. Always a moneyspinner this one. All that is needed is a load of small prizes, either donated, or purchased cheaply at one of the wholesalers who specialise in this sort of thing, and away you go.

We had a tombola stall at many of the events, and I am sure that the prizes just go round in circles, with the winners on one occasion donating them at the next! However all that matters is that it works, and the profits always come in.

TREASURE HUNT

A great favourite with the children. One was organised on a summer Sunday, and 58 children turned up, accompanied by 74 adults and the odd dog or two. They were all given a set of clues and a map, and a list of 'Treasures' to collect on the way round. The route took them through Meanwood Park, The Hollies, and Meanwood Woods and eventually to the garden at The Myrtle Tavern on Parkside Road. It took most of them about one and a half hours, and they were ready for the nice barbecue that awaited them. In addition to collecting items, they had to fill in the question sheet that contained items such as 'How many chimney stacks on Hustlers Row?' (A row of old quarrymen's cottages in the woods), and 'Where is the crocodile?' (A large rock in the beck). The winners received prizes of course, and M.S.B.A. won to the tune of £176.

TABLE TOP SALE

The ladies of the Mother's Union at the Church put on a sale in the Hall. Their tables were laden with everything that was saleable, and a tidy donation to the funds was received.

TEAS IN THE GARDEN

On a number of nice weekend afternoons we provided teas in the garden at Ivy Cottage. We didn't make a fortune but every little helps. No fixed charges were made, but the donation jars were around!

VICTORIAN WALK

Arthur Hopwood took a party of walkers on a tour of the area, all of who were eager to hear his tales about old Meanwood. They finished up in the Chapel schoolroom for a nice supper laid on by Marjorie Hopwood and Heather Clark. At the end we were £105 nearer our target. No matter how many times Arthur arranges these walks they always draw a crowd.

WALKS

See Sponsorship chapter for details.

WINEWALKS

Of all the ways to spend a nice summer's evening, and at the same time raise money for a good cause, winewalks must surely be near the top of the list. They were always very popular, and proven by the frequently heard comment when one was coming to an end. "When is the next one?"

A bit hectic on the night, but fairly easy to organise beforehand. On the "profit to effort" test they scored highly. Someone once described them as "Posh pub crawls." I wouldn't quite agree, but it was not too far off the mark! The first requirement is to find three volunteers who are prepared to open up their house for an evening and serve drinks. Ideally, but not essential, the house should be fairly large and have a decent sized garden. The three of them should be within reasonable walking distance of each other. If they are too far apart it puts off some of the older people, and if too close the guests haven't time to sober up between visits!. We had some very interesting visits to private houses, and also used the Parochial Hall and the Meanwood Institute on occasions.

Tickets were sold beforehand at the very modest price of £3 a head. On the night guests could start anytime after seven o'clock. (In many cases this was interpreted as 7.01 p.m.!) They would start at whichever venue they wished, and have one free glass of wine and a chinwag before moving on to the next place, and so on. If anyone wanted more than the one free glass at each house it was available at the cash bar. Nuts and crisps were sold at each venue to help things along, together with a raffle or silly little moneymaking game such as 'How many peas in the jar?'

For obvious reasons driving was strictly banned for the wine drinkers, and we insisted that everyone walked. Teetotallers were not given any excuse to miss out on the evening's fun as soft drinks were always available. In fact it was surprising how many stuck to the fruit drinks. There were various theories put forward as to the best way to navigate around. Some said the best way was to start at the farthest point from home, and others insisted the opposite direction was better, so that you could sober up on the walk back. Another theory was that bearing in mind that Meanwood is quite hilly, it was best to start at the highest house and work your way downhill. We never did reach a consensus, which was a good thing, because we did not want everyone at the same house at the same time. The third house was where the guests usually settled down for some serious drinking and tale telling. It was not unknown for the third host to have to call 'time' at long past midnight, particularly when the event was on a Saturday night.

The secret of making a good profit was to obtain all the wine as cheaply as possible, or better still for free! We were very fortunate in that a friend of mine, who was an old Meanwood lad, ran a large wine importing business, and was extremely generous to M.S.B.A. in several ways. One telephone call was all that was required to bring him to the door with a few dozen bottles in his boot. We never knew what to expect, but there was always a wide selection of good samples, and all sorts of odds and ends to tempt the palate. In addition to these we received various gifts from individuals, and these ranged from well-known brands to some rather dubious 'Homemades' (The 'Sycamore Sap' proved rather unpopular, but as one of my sons had made it, it wasn't too embarrassing pouring it down the sink!)

Early on in the campaign we persuaded the Parents Association to buy a bulk quantity of wine and beer glasses and tumblers. A wise move, which saved us a lot of hire costs and was very convenient. These, together with wine, soft drinks, nuts and crisps were distributed to the three hosts the night before the event. We soon found by experience the average amount of the various drinks consumed, but we always allowed a good margin on top of this for safety. I hate to think what would have happened if we had run out of anything half way through the evening! At the end of the evening we sold off the part-bottles, and put the rest in the cellar ready for the next one.

We built up a list of the regular clientele, and never had a problem in selling tickets. The numbers ranged from about 75 to 125. All told we held six walks and this brought in net profits of £1,811.

CHECKLIST

Each house will require the following;

Wine. Work on the basis that the average person will consume one glass (Those who do not drink wine will be balanced by the ones who drink more than one glass).

Work on getting 7 glasses per litre.

Ratio of white to red of about 2 to 1.

Add a good safety margin. The surplus will do for the next one.

Soft Drinks. Have a good selection. We found the good quality types in cartons the most popular.

Nuts, and a variety of plain and flavoured crisps.

Buckets and ice for cooling the white wine.

Raffle or game prizes, and tickets.

Wine glasses and tumblers.

Bottle opener and corkscrew. Vital!

Scissors for the cartons, and to cut a third off the ticket each time a free drink was taken.

Table and cloth for bar.

Cash float, and cashbox.

Notice re bar and other prices.

Notice about forthcoming events.

Notice to put outside the gate.

Last but not least, a good and sober barman!

I hope you have as jolly a time as we did.

14
FURTHER IDEAS TO CONSIDER

Lots of ideas were put forward to the Committee to consider, but for various reasons not all of them were adopted. In some cases they were thought to be unsuitable, others were too big to tackle, on others we couldn't find a volunteer to take it on, or quite simply we just ran out of time before the target was reached, and the Community became fed up to the teeth with events!

Readers looking for new ideas however may pick up a few here.
Antiques Road Show.
Bed Push (A Sponsored event).
Bridge evening.
Book Fair (Plus records, tapes, and C.D.'s).
Cow Pat Lottery.
Christmas Day Fast!
Country and Western evening.
Duck Race on the beck (Plastic variety!)
Flower, vegetable, wine making and brewing competition/show.
Foreign coins and banknotes collection.
Gamble for a car (Throw six sixes, but remember to take out insurance!)
Gateau eating contest. (Our minutes record "This suggestion by Martin Cockerill was received as a sick joke by Committee members and did not proceed."
Houses of Parliament trip.
Ice cream trail. (On the lines of a winewalk)
Karaoke evening.
Knobbly knees competition.
Local recipe book.

Maggot Racing.
Model railway exhibition.
Mad Hatters tea party.
Pancake race.
Parachuting. (Sponsored).
Spaghetti eating competition.
Sponsored Mountain Climb.
Hire a train for a shopping trip to London or France prior to Christmas.
Seaside outing by coach or train.
Strawberry Fayre.
Sponsored Hymn Singing.
Skipathon.
Whist Drives.
Worm charming contest.
Yorkshire Pudding race.

I am sure there are lots more!

Keep trying, it's surprising how sometimes the daftest ideas come up trumps.

15
MISCELLANY

FILMING RIGHTS

After the children and staff had moved out of the old School, and before it was handed over to the builders, there were a few months when it was all empty. Somehow Yorkshire Television got wind of this, and approached us to see if we would allow them to use it for filming some scenes for the current series of "Darling Buds of May". They went on to say there would be a fee payable to the school of £500 per time and they wanted to come twice. We did not need to deliberate too much before giving them our decision!

In addition to the welcome cash, there was a lot of local excitement generated, and there were always crowds of children (and adults) peering over the wall when the cameras rolled up. The old tennis courts, which are now the playground, were crammed full of generators, caravans for dressers and costumes, canteens and miles of cables everywhere. The old schoolyard was also crammed with dozens of film extras, floodlights, scaffolding and more miles of cables.

What everyone wanted of course, was get a glimpse of the stars, David Jason ('Pa') and Pam Ferris ('Ma'). They were not disappointed, and indeed David in particular would often go across to the wall and chat to the children and sign autographs. The stars also signed a quantity of wooden souvenirs for us to sell (see Sales chapter).

The inside of the main hall had been transformed by the scenery people into the Village Hall in the story. It was amazing how quickly and realistically they did so. They built a wooden stage at one end, and made hardboard frames to change the shape of the windows, and with a few pots of emulsion paint the place was changed beyond recognition in two or three days. The Hall backs onto Green Road, so that every time the cameras were about to roll, a message was relayed to a man outside in the road to stop the traffic and prevent any unwanted background noise. The passing motorists were very co-operative, and even the children were hushed by his signals.

The crowd obviously could not see what was going on in the Hall, much to their disappointment, but I must admit to pulling rank and going in to watch one session. It was very interesting. One scene however was shot outside and gave everyone a good view. This was a night-time scene, supposedly at Christmas, and David Jason rolled up in his old blue lorry with Santa Claus hidden under a tarpaulin. Santa had to be smuggled into the Village Hall, and as it was supposed to be snowing, a large 'cherrypicker' crane was brought in with a man on top. His sole task was to sprinkle what appeared to be soapflakes down on the scene. When it was shown on television it all looked very wintry indeed. Incidentally all this activity, involving dozens of actors, actresses and equipment was condensed to a few minutes on screen. The mind boggles at the cost of the full episode. Nobody grumbled though, as M.S.B.A. did very well out of it all, even topping up the fees by having a refreshment stall outside Ivy Cottage!

Some time later Yorkshire Television made another film in Meanwood. This time it was for the series 'A Touch of Frost', and it was all shot at night around the Mausoleum in the churchyard. They paid a fee of £750 this time, and although it went to the Church, they kindly passed it all on to M.S.B.A. Another nice boost. All told therefore we made £1,750 out of filming rights with virtually no effort on our part.

WORLD CUP

Yes, we even made money out of the world cup in the summer of 1990. A parent very generously gave us a ticket for the Cup Final, to raffle, sell, or use however we could to benefit the funds. I approached John Morgan, the sports columnist at the Yorkshire Evening Post, to see if he would publicise it for us. He did better than that, he had a contact (the owner of the 'Flying Pizza' in Street Lane) who bought it for £500. Thanks John!

WEDDING CATERING

A couple who were going to be married in Meanwood Parish Church, and have their reception at St. Chad's in Headingley, said that if a team of ladies were interested in doing all the catering work they would pay £300 into M.S.B.A. Now that was a bit different to our normal fundraising activities, but a few telephone calls later it was all laid on. I thought it was easy money, but the ladies who did it all enlightened me in no uncertain fashion, and said every penny had been hard earned. Well-done ladies!

TO BE 'BEWELLED'

One Sunday morning whilst telling the congregation about the latest state of the Appeal funds, the Vicar, Richard Wiggen, said a new word had been coined in Meanwood. It was 'Bewelled.'

Its meaning was to be cornered by yours truly, and either sold a ticket for the latest raffle, a ticket for the next event, coerced into doing a job, persuaded into making something or just be badgered into doing something for the Appeal. I was not sure whether to be dismayed or overjoyed when hearing about this, but I must admit that when I walked into various meetings, remarks such as "What are you conning us for today?" or "Look out he's here again" were becoming the norm. Certain other comments have been censored. I also understand that the Men's Society defined 'A Bewell' as a new unit of currency, which was the amount of money you knew you would have to part with when I walked in!

MATHS STANDARDS

Whilst removing some old built-in cupboards (to sell of course) from the room that is now occupied by year six I came across an old writing slate. We believe that the use of these slates in the School ceased about 1920, so we saved it as a memento of those old pre pen and ink days. What proved to be even more interesting however was a faded old piece of card that I found in all the accumulated dust and rubbish. It was entitled 'The Northern Criterion Test Card'. On one side there were test questions for Standard V1, and on the reverse for Standard V11. There was no indication of the date, except that one of the questions referred to Crowns, so that probably puts it earlier than 1902.

I wrote to the Editor of *The Times* newspaper hoping we might get some publicity, but alas, despite a number of hopeful telephone conversations it all came to nothing. I think the truth was that they could not answer the questions. Can YOU? Try this one for a start;

"What sum of money will amount to £562 in 7years and 2 months at three and a half percent?" or how about this. "A puts £30 into a business, B puts £50, and C £80. In the first half year they gain 40% upon their capital. In the second half year they lose £15. They then dissolve the partnership, and each takes what belongs to him. How much should each receive?"

Did you manage it? (Without a calculator of course.)

THE PARENT'S ASSOCIATION

The Association wholeheartedly supported M.S.B.A. throughout the three and a half years, in all sorts of ways, but their fundraising really started 26 years prior to the latest Appeal being launched. Talk of the rebuilding and extension of the School had gone on for as long as anyone could remember. My wife who was on the Committee 26 years ago tells me that they decided to start the ball rolling by putting aside 10% of all the profits each year into a special rebuilding fund. Unfortunately none of those parents saw any benefits for their children, but probably many of them are now reaping the rewards of their foresight through their grandchildren. This annual 10% share, plus interest, steadily mounted, so that when M.S.B.A. was started they gave us a flying start with a cheque for £2,600, and contributions of £1,400 were received later.

The Association organised many events specifically for M.S.B.A. and was a major force throughout the Appeal.

THE PAROCHIAL CHURCH COUNCIL

The P.C.C. helped in giving the Appeal a good send-off by contributing the balance of the old School House rent account (£2,000). In addition to their general support they staged specific events such as the Autumn Fair and the Flower Festival that made significant profits for the Appeal.

THE MEANWOOD INSTITUTE

Nothing to do with the School Appeal at all, but to show readers that once you have started charity fundraising it is difficult to stop! The Institute is a little old building only a couple of hundred of yards from the School, and dates back to the early part of the last century. I suppose that in today's language it would be called a community centre. It had fallen into a very bad state of repair, and almost reached the point of no return, when the only Trustee approached me to see if I could give any advice regarding one of the century-old snooker tables which was sinking into the floor. I checked, and sure enough it had sunk through the rotten damp old floorboards and the few old pensioners who still played there on an afternoon were having to 'aim off' to counteract the slope!

That was the beginning of another long story. Suffice it to say here that some of the members of the Meanwood Trinity Men's Society and others, decided to do something about the building before it was too late. A Committee was formed and fundraising began all over again in Meanwood. Well, it never stopped really, because this all started just as the School Appeal was drawing to a close. At first we did not realise the seriousness of the state of the building, but it soon became apparent that major works were required.

It differed from the School Appeal in that all the work was carried out by volunteers, most of who were early retired men like myself. Fund-raising followed the now well known pattern, with winewalks, sales, walks, jumble sales, and even another 'Snookerthon'. All told we raised £23,000 which was sufficient to complete the work.

CHAPEL STAINED GLASS WINDOWS

About the same time as the Institute Appeal, the main stained glass windows in the Chancel area of the Methodist Church required urgent attention. In fact, they had to be removed and completely rebuilt by a specialist. To raise the money to pay for this I borrowed an idea from School, the dedicated giving scheme. I counted how many small panes there were in the windows, and discovered there were 1,853.

We put out an appeal for panes to be sponsored at £2 each, and very soon enough money was in to carry out the work. The idea seemed to tickle people's fancy, and they can now gaze upon the finished windows and see the results of their generosity. In a similar manner to the lady who wanted to know which was her dedicated stone at School, somebody wanted to know precisely which window panes they had sponsored. In this case it was the Brownie leader, so we decided to tell the girls that it was a particular panel on one of the windows, and they were delighted. They now, quite rightly, consider that section to be theirs.

16
CONCLUSION

How on earth do you sum up something that has taken over your life for nearly four years? Was all the blood, sweat and tears really worth it? There can only be one answer to those questions, and that is a very emphatic YES.

To see the School today, with the 210 children working and playing in the environment of the new buildings is proof and reward enough.

It was only made possible by the thousands of hours of work put in by dedicated Committee members, and many others, and the full support of the Community. It has been a great privilege and pleasure for me to lead such a venture.

Many local people have been named in this book, but inevitably not every supporter made it into print. If your name did not appear, please forgive the omission, but rest assured your contribution to the Appeal in whatever form it took, was much appreciated.

It just proves what can be achieved if a Community pulls together in a just common cause. Old divisions between the Churches and other groups disappeared, and the effect will surely last for a long, long time. I certainly hope so. Friendships that were forged in those days will continue for evermore.

All the workers were volunteers, and not only gave of their time and talents, but in many cases their cash as well. Nobody claimed any expenses.

I must also pay tribute to the partners and children of all the Committee members, and in particular to my own wife Christine, who put in so much hard work behind the scenes. They had to tolerate our frequent long absences at Committee meetings and events, and I am sure that they also put lots of good ideas into our heads to pass off as our own at the meetings. In addition to that, of course, many of them worked hard at the events.

There were, of course, times of great frustration, and disappointments, and more than once there was the temptation to pack it all in, and "Let the

Government pay for it all" as someone initially suggested. Thankfully we resisted the temptation, and stuck it out, but I can assure you there were a few near misses!

We also had our moments of sadness and joy during our times together. Don Prentis, a member of the Committee, died on May 12th. 1992, but not until he had made a significant contribution in approaching charities and industry, and soliciting a number of private donations. Glynis Shaw, one of the early stalwarts, left the area to go and live in Wales in May 1990. Our joy came when Doreen Wood our film-maker remarried, but she was very considerate, and didn't cause any problems with the records, as she kept the same surname by marrying her late husband's brother! After the Appeal was finished, I was asked to be a Governor of the School. I am not sure whether that was a punishment or a reward, but I was delighted to accept.

I will always remember the last fundraising event, which was a Quiz Night and the drawing of the last big raffle. It took place on November 28th. 1992 in the Parochial Hall, the scene of so many memorable times, and it was obvious then that we would reach our target in a matter of days. There were a few closing speeches, and many people were quite emotional about coming to the end of it all. When the actual day dawned when we reached the magical figure of £150,000 on December 18th. we were all expecting to be over the moon, but strange as it may seem most of us felt it to be a bit of an anti-climax. I certainly did, and after ringing round to tell everyone I just slumped in the chair!

After it was all over, and we were analysing the accounts, we realised what a large proportion of our income had been derived from drinking, eating and gambling. Sad perhaps, but a fact that fundraisers cannot ignore.

We were all delighted some months later when the School took first place in the Altered Building Category of the 1993 Leeds Awards for Architecture, and the following year received a Commendation in the National Civic Trust Awards.

I think it may be appropriate to reprint here the words of the Headteacher, Bryn Evans, which he wrote for an article in the final Newsletter.

> *'The last three and a half years have passed by remarkably quickly for me, perhaps because I have never attended so many Quiz Nights, Dances, Greek nights, Sponsored Events of one kind or another, nor participated in quite so many raffles! Apart from one or two occasions when things didn't go according to plan I have enjoyed all the M.S.B.A. events.*
>
> *Two things stand out for me; the way in which the various organisations and churches in Meanwood have come together in support of M.S.B.A., and the*

incredible generosity of so many people. Those of us lucky enough to work in the magnificent new building will never be able to say "THANK YOU" enough to the community for such unstinting support. But from this Spring we will be trying as hard as we can to use the building to good effect for the express benefit of the children, thereby acting out our "Thank You." '

This magnificent fund raising effort has secured the education for several next generations of Meanwood children, and the creation of a school worthy of its inhabitants, both now and in the future—perhaps the greatest achievement of all. As Christopher Beckett might have done 152 years ago, we too can congratulate ourselves quietly on a job well done."

I do not pretend that we had a magic formula and got everything right. Far from it, but one thing we did get out of it all was a sense of satisfaction at the end of the day.

I trust that the local readers will have enjoyed reliving many of the events of those years. Readers from further afield, to whom Meanwood is merely a strange name, will, I hope, have gleaned a little from the preceding pages that may help them in their own fundraising activities. If so, I will be delighted.

It is very difficult to sum up advice in a few words, but I will try;

THINK BIG, AND BE 100% COMMITTED TO THE TASK.
SET TARGETS, AND STRIVE TO BETTER THEM.
WHATEVER YOU DO, DO CHEERFULLY.
ALWAYS GIVE PEOPLE VALUE FOR THEIR MONEY.
BE CREATIVE.
BE, ABOVE ALL, ENTHUSIASTIC IN ALL YOU DO.
ALWAYS BE OPTIMISTIC.
IF IT GOES WRONG, KEEP COOL.
ALWAYS THANK YOUR HELPERS AND DONORS.

Finally may I say THANK YOU to everyone who contributed in any way whatsoever to the success of THE MEANWOOD SCHOOL BUILDING APPEAL. The success came about thanks to the hard work and contributions from many people. It came in many forms, some in cash, some by way of gifts of time and talents. Whether your contribution came by masterminding a big event, or humbly washing up afterwards, or quietly attending in the car park, it was a vital part of the whole, and we could not have done what we did without it.

Our reward can be seen at the end of Green Road, a fitting legacy from today's people for tomorrow's children, and . . .

WE DID IT OUR WAY!

17
APPENDICES

A History of the School.

M.S.B.A. Patrons and Committee.

The Professionals.

Analysis of the fundraising.

Useful Names and Addresses.

Architects drawing and description.

Notes of new ideas

A HISTORY OF THE SCHOOL

The founder of the School was Christopher Beckett Esq. He was born on January 25th 1777, the second son of Sir John Beckett Bart of Gledhow Hall. He had seven brothers and three sisters. Christopher Beckett was a banker in Leeds and for a number of years a magistrate of the West Riding. He was also a benefactor, leading trustee and administrator of many public charities. He went on to serve as the Deputy Lieutenant of the West Riding and was Mayor of Leeds in 1819 and 1829.

The School he founded in 1840 consisted of the old schoolroom, a classroom, and the Master's house. The old schoolroom is of special architectural interest and is, with the rest of the School, a Grade Two listed building. The room that is presently occupied by year six has an unusual belfry tower that surmounts the original entrance-way to the building. It can be seen today from the newly named Beckett Court. The Green Road elevation has early English gothic windows and some finely carved heads on the corbels under the gutters which have never been identified. In fact the original plans of the School and the architect's name have all been lost.

The Meanwood Hall Estate (now Meanwood Park Hospital) was purchased by Christopher Beckett in 1824 from Robert Denison. Later he bought additional land in Meanwood as it came on the market. In 1837 he acquired some land from the successors of Francis Whalley deceased, a local tanner, which included a few stone cottages, a stone quarry and some woodland (part of Meanwood Woods). The site of Christopher Beckett's School was the southern part of this land called Low Walker's Close that was bounded on the South side by Woodside Road (Green Road). The School was built of local stone, possibly from the quarries of Messrs Daniel and Dunbar, who a few years later provided stone for the Parish Church.

The School was the personal property of Christopher Beckett; he maintained it and paid for the staff until his death in 1847. It was in that year that the Parish of Meanwood was formed out of the chapelries of Chapel Allerton and Headingley and it is almost certain that the School was used for worship until the Parish Church was built in 1849.

In 1848 Sir Thomas Beckett Bart and his sisters Mary and Elizabeth, conveyed the building to the Rev. George Urquhart, Incumbent of Meanwood, and his successors. The deed recites Christopher Beckett's intention to provide education for the children of the poor, resident in or near the village, and the wish of Sir Thomas and his sisters to perpetuate the benevolent design of the founder. The deed also refers to the gift of £1,000 made by Mary and Elizabeth, the income from which was to be used to provide the stipends of the staff, defray the expenses of maintenance and the cost of equipment. Provision was made for the School to be used on Sundays and also by adults.

The School was to be conducted according to the aims and designs of The Incorporated National Society and upon the principles of the Established Church, religious and moral instruction being under the sole direction of the incumbent.

William Beckett Denison became a trustee in 1864, the deed of appointment relating the deaths of Mary and Elizabeth who had each left £750 to the Meanwood National School Endowment Fund.

Eight years later Sir Thomas, under an Act authorising the Conveyance and Endowment of Sites for Schools, gave a further portion of Low Walker's Close on which the Infants' School was built, very probably with financial assistance of the Beckett family.

Early in the 1870's Mr.M.W.Nicholson was appointed headmaster, a post he held for about thirty five years. He was responsible for many improvements in the lot of the villagers and was for a time a church warden.

Grants paid to the School Managers were dependant on the child's success in examinations and on registrations. The early log books faithfully record inspections. Attendance levels and performance in the three R's (Reading, wRiting, and aRithmetic) were carefully noted.

In 1876 a special licence enabled a marriage ceremony to be conducted in the School whilst the Parish Church was being extended by the provision of the South aisle.

In 1889 a further classroom was needed. An appeal was made to Miss Mary Beckett of Somerby Park, Gainsborough, a daughter of Sir Thomas and she headed the subscription list with £50. The addition was completed in 1890 at the Green Road end of the Infants' School, (the present kitchen) leaving an outstanding debt of £70. Perhaps a further appeal was made to Miss Beckett, for in October she is recorded as having given £100 and in the following month she came to Meanwood to present the Infants' School prizes.

It is believed that a charge of 2d. a week was made at the time. One must wonder if it was collected in every case. The Elementary Education Act of 1891 was adopted by the Managers and thereafter attendance was free, but parents were asked to contribute six to ten shillings a year voluntarily. The Yorkshire Penny Bank introduced a scheme to encourage thrift and by 1892 sixty-four accounts had been opened by children attending the School. (There are still about fifty accounts held by today's children at the Yorkshire Bank, continuing the century old link.)

A new cloakroom was built in 1892 and in 1912 an additional room was erected over the classroom adjacent the main hall. This is now the Bewell Room.

It is interesting to read the comments of two of the Headmasters. The first one is an extract from the Parish Magazine of 1949:

> *'Pursuing its course unobtrusively and with few outstanding events to mark its way, the school has played a not unimportant part in the Christian life of the village.*
>
> *Perhaps one or two memories may be of interest. The even tenor of our way was once disturbed by an official visit of the Lord Mayor. It proved to be a very stimulating event. How the children worked to produce something worthy of His Worship's commendation. All enjoyed the occasion, and none more thoroughly than Leeds' first citizen.*
>
> *A Memorable day was that on which we were addressed by Commander Carpenter, V.C. of H.M.S. Vindictive and Zeebrugge fame. We were most thrilled as we listened to a gallant naval hero and a very modest English gentleman.*
>
> *On September 1st. 1939 scholars and staff were evacuated to Knaresborough. What lay ahead of us? As we departed from Meanwood this question seemed part of the air we breathed. Lessons at the new school soon became the normal routine, but the call of home was persistent and by the end of the year most of us were again in Leeds.*
>
> *By 1940 we were at work in our usual classrooms, the late Colonel Kitson Clark having generously provided us with an air raid shelter at Meanwoodside.*
>
> *At this time many 'old boys' then serving in H.M.Forces visited the school. Happy and interesting chats with the children were frequent and enjoyable. Later we were to remember with sorrow and pride 'old boys' who had fallen.*
>
> *In 1946 the beech tree at the upper side of the playground was struck by lightning. The boys are pleased that sufficient of its stump to serve for three still survives.*
>
> *Some years ago the school provided a Maid of Honour to the 'Queen of Children's Day'. In 1947 it provided the 'Queen,' Pamela Hopper, who occupied this exalted position with conspicuous charm and ability.*
>
> *Many of our children won scholarships under the old system of award. Under the new system we continue to do well. In 1948 fifteen children succeeded in gaining admission to secondary schools. This year, from a smaller number of entrants, ten pupils met with success.'*

F. COOK

The second extract is from an article written by the current Headteacher, Bryn Evans, in the school's 150th. Anniversary Brochure.

'From our vantage point in 1990 it is tempting to speculate on Christopher Beckett's motive. Did he have thoughts of leaving the school as a 'monument' for future generations? Or was the building of the school carried out to meet a real need? There is certainly evidence of poverty and ill health in Meanwood during the last century and Christopher Beckett's name can be found amongst those who regularly contributed towards relief for the poor.

I see Beckett as a far-sighted individual, one who had deep concerns for the needs of the children of Meanwood village. I am certain that his was a genuine concern for the welfare of the children of the poor. The building of the school was his way of trying to better the lot of these children by providing an education which would prepare them for the world of work.

If Christopher Beckett could travel forward in time to the present day I'm certain he would recognise the school and master's house quite easily! What he would find difficult to comprehend would be the resources available in the school. Apart from the wealth of colourful pictures, story, and reference books, such things as televisions, video recorders, radios, calculators, tape recorders, computers, disc drives, printers, and V.D.U's . . . would I'm sure be completely baffling to him. Yet all these are things which the modern primary child takes for granted in the classroom. Such tools are as familiar to our children as slates and chalks would have been to the Victorian child. Perhaps the child-centered approach of the modern primary school would amaze him just as much as the technology; perhaps the absence of the cane would too!'

****

In more recent times a new toilet block was built in the 1960's in the playground. This was a great improvement, but the children still had to cross the yard in all weathers to reach it.

The timetable of the recent development was;

December 1988.	Permission granted by L.E.A. and D.F.E. to proceed.
March 1989.	Appeal Committee formed.
June 23rd. 1989.	Official launch of fundraising campaign.
July 14th. 1991.	The School closed, and moved to Bentley Primary.
March 2nd. 1992.	The Contractors moved onto site.
December 18th.1992.	Target of £150,000 reached.
March 29th. 1993.	The building was completed.
April 24th. 1993.	The School re-opened to everyone's delight.

During the works we kept a good eye open for any items of interest that might come to light, but apart from the Victorian writing slate and the test card found behind an old cupboard, we were disappointed.

The Contractors, however, discovered a well during the excavations. It was about 25 foot deep and beautifully lined with curved bricks. It was situated right where they had to place one of the foundation bases for the Hall extension and caused a hold-up whilst the Engineer decided what to do with it. In the end it was filled and capped with reinforced concrete. Arthur Hopwood made a thorough inspection before they did so, but alas nothing of interest could be dredged up.

M.S.B.A. PATRONS

The Rt. Worshipful The Lord Mayor of the City of Leeds.

Councillors Les Carter, Bill Kilgallon, Ronald Feldman, Denise Atkinson

Lord Grimthorpe O.B.E., D.L.

The Rt. Rev. D.N. de L. Young M.A. Bishop of Ripon.

Dr. Keith Hampson M.P.

M.S.B.A. COMMITTEE

Served throughout

Peter Bewell	*Chairman*		
Barbara Blakeney			
Jackie Brewer			
Anne Burgess	*Deputy Headteacher*		
Bryn Evans	*Headteacher*		
Arthur Hopwood			
Ian Jackson			
Alan Pedley			
Cathy Stevens	*Secretary*		
Janet Thornton			
Doreen Wood			

Heather Booth *Staff (Sub-Comm)*
Margaret Leiper *Co-opted Minute Secr'ty*

Served part of the period

Carolina Brook
Steve Clemmens
Martin Cockerill
Brian Coulthard *Treasurer*
Chris Croft Staff
Stanley Dodd *Vicar*
Frank Dunderdale
Vanessa Garner
Brian Glassby
Geoff Holland *Treasurer*
Christine Holmes
Susan Houghton
Alan Menzies *Auditor*
Janice Moutsakis
Don Prentis
Glynis Shaw
Bev Simpson
Gordon Simpson
Peter Smithson
Jon Stevens
Richard Wiggen Vicar
Elaine Wilson

THE PROFESSIONALS

The residents of Meanwood, and the Governors in particular, would like to express their sincere thanks to all the building team, from the Architect who conceived the ideas, to the labourers on site.

The finished School is a credit to them all.

ARCHITECTS   JONES & STOCKS.

MAIN CONTRACTORS   SHEPHERD CONSTRUCTION

QUANTITY SURVEYORS   THE M.T.L. PARTNERSHIP

CONSULTING ENGINEERS   BAILEY & WRIGHT

***

The Building took first place in the Altered Buildings Category of the 1993 Leeds Awards for Architecture.

***

A commendation in the National Civic Trust Awards followed in 1994.

ANALYSIS OF THE FUNDRAISING

	£
Donations from individuals (including Covenants & G.A.Y.E.)	26,739
Donations from Industry and Commerce	6,390
Donations from Charities and other Churches	19,393
Donations & events by Local Groups including our Church and School	19,771
Events run by the Appeal & Individuals, including Raffles and Sponsored events	43,992
Sales run by the Appeal and Individuals	2,945
Bank Interest and Tax reclaimed from Covenants	27,548
Scrap, Smartie Tubes, 100 Club, Stamps, Coupons and Acorns	6,392
TOTAL RAISED	**153,170**
Less expenses	**3,170**
	£150,000

The £10,000 from the estate of Lord Allerton is included in Donations from Charities and other churches.

After the target was reached the fund continued to grow, and at the time of writing (January 1996) stands at over £162,000.

SOME USEFUL NAMES AND ADDRESSES

The Directory of Social Change
Radius Works, Back Lane,
London NW3 1HL
An excellent organisation that runs training courses, and publishes material on charities, trusts, and the like.
Write for latest lists.

The West Riding Charities Information Bureau.
11, Upper York Street,
Wakefield,
WF1 3LQ
There are similar Bureaus in other areas.

Charity Commission.
St. Alban's House
57-60 Haymarket
London SW1Y 4QX

Charities Aid Foundation,
48 Pembury Road,
Tonbridge,
Kent,
TN9 2JD

Inland Revenue.
Contact the local office for all the latest leaflets on charitable giving schemes, etc.

'MEANWOOD' The excellent little history book by
Arthur Hopwood and Fred Casperson.
Available from;
W.A.Hopwood,
44 Parkside Crescent,
Meanwood, Leeds LS6 4JU
£2.95 plus 50p P&P

NOTE: *The Authors have very generously agreed that all proceeds from the sales of this book will be given to the Meanwood School Building Appeal.*

FUNdraising, 'WE DID IT OUR WAY!'

Further copies available from;

BEWCRAFT
Ivy Cottage,
95, Green Road,
Meanwood,
Leeds LS6 4LE

DONATIONS

The Meanwood School Building Appeal remains open indefinitely to raise further funds for developing the School, and the building of a nursery unit. Donations will always be welcome.

Cheques payable to 'M.S.B.A.'
The Headteacher
Meanwood C.of E (Aided) Primary School,
Green Road,
Meanwood,
Leeds LS6 4LD.   Thank You.

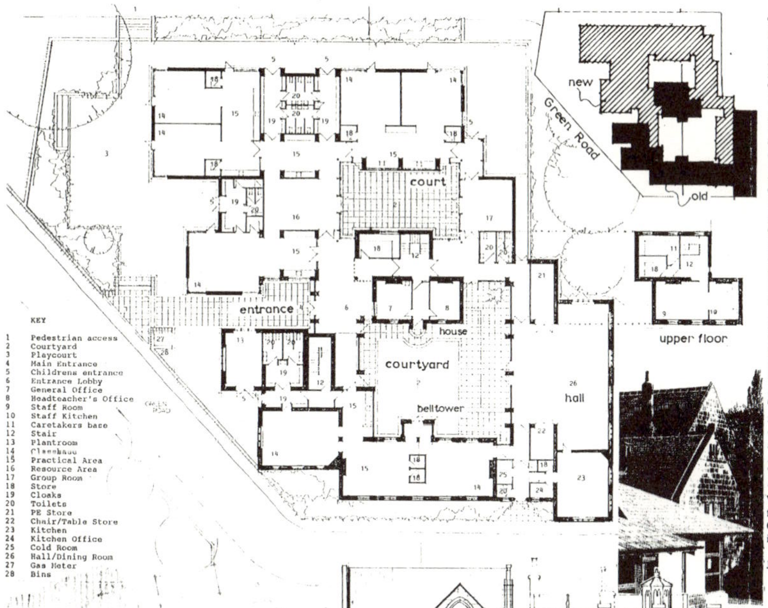

The development of the site has consisted of the complete refurbishment of the old Listed School Buildings along with a doubling of floor space through the construction of extensive new-build additions. This has created a one-form entry primary school catering for 210 pupils in seven year-groups, in the age-range 5 to 11 years.

The new-build accommodation provides a self-contained suite for the reception year and a further four classrooms with a range of shared practical spaces, resource areas, library and group room. Classrooms for the two upper years are contained within the existing buildings and here further practical and resource areas are equipped for more advanced work.

Conversion work has also provided a new hall and kitchen for the preparation of school meals.

The derelict Master's House has been refurbished as staff and administrative accommodation and a new entrance hall is attached to one side.

Toilets, cloakrooms, storage space, cleaner's stores etc are arranged in small clusters and distributed throughout the complex, local to the various classroom groupings.

The new-build elements take the form of small inter-linked pavilions of single storey, woven around a system of enclosed courtyards and recreation areas which provide outdoor space for work and play. The new building-forms are low and spreading, deliberately held down to the scale of their young occupants : they do not seek to emulate their Victorian neighbours but are complementary in their scale and detailing and in the use of natural stone and slate for walls and roofs. Great emphasis is placed on daylighting and thermal efficiency and the interiors are constructed in robust but friendly materials which do not require onerous maintenance.

The redundant tennis courts to the north have been repaired and re-fenced to provide a new playground, adjacent to which there is an enclosed area of grass and trees for recreation and environmental study. The reception year has its own smaller play area with planted margins and views out towards the space where parents gather. Throughout there is a high standard of landscaping to produce an emphasis on a green environment.

Work on site started in early 1992, and was complete in Spring 1993, following which the building took first place in the Altered Buildings Category of the 1993 Leeds Awards for Architecture : a commendation in the National Civic Trust Awards followed in 1994.

Jones + Stocks Architects.   January 1996

Architects Plans and description

126

NOTES OF NEW IDEAS

Make a note here of any further ideas for fundraising that you discover.

NOTES